HOW TO DOUBLE YOUR SALES IN
6 WEEKS

BRUCE KING

Ecademy Press

How to Double your Sales in 6 WEEKS
© Bruce King 2008

Book Cover Design & Typesetting by Martin Coote
martincoote@googlemail.com

Cover Photograph: Guillermo Perales Gonzalez/iStockPhoto

Set in *Delicious 10.5 on 14pt* a typeface by Jos Buivenga

First published in 2008 by;

Ecademy Press

6 Woodland Rise, Penryn,

Cornwall UK TR10 8QD

info@ecademy-press.com

www.ecademy-press.com

Printed and Bound by;
Lightning Source in the UK and USA

Printed on acid-free paper from managed forests. This book is printed on demand, so no copies will be remaindered or pulped.

ISBN 978-1-905823-38-3

PRAISE FOR

HOW TO DOUBLE YOUR SALES IN 6 WEEKS

"This is THE sales book for everyone and especially those who spend too much time looking outside of themselves and overlook their innate personal strengths! Especially good focus and practical tips on how to get that "inner sales knowledge" working and simple ways to follow through. Thank you Bruce for putting me back on track."

PAULINE CRAWFORD
Managing Director, Corporate Heart, putting 'life' back into business—mapping professional behaviour to turbo-charge business back to life!

"This is a 'must-have' business book for the sole trader, budding entrepreneur and serious salesperson. They will benefit greatly from understanding and applying its excellent methods and systems. Tried and tested, pragmatic and straightforward—the wisdom of years related to success for the modern day. Keep it away from your competitors."

STEVE MCNULTY
Chairman of 'The Board' —
The UK's Prestigious Executive Business Club

"Bruce King's well-researched book challenges your current mind-set on the fastest way to close that deal. His proven strategy and sales-efficient tactics show you how to make every day of the week a highly profitable one—for both your customers and yourself."

CAROLE SPIERS
International authority on Corporate Stress, BBC Broadcaster.
Author of best-selling Tolley's 'Managing Stress in the Workplace' and 'Turn Your Passion into Profit.

"Wow! Made me feel young and excited again and continuously reminded me why I love selling. Definitely worth reading and implementing the valuable lessons learnt in 'How To Double Your Sales in 6 Weeks'."

ABHI NAHA
VP of Global Sales for Idem and Chairman of the Beatbullying Charity.

"This book is both captivating and extremely rich! The author delivers on all levels. I highly recommend this to any sales executive looking for the edge!"

CRAIG GOLDBLATT
Author of The Oscar Principles

"So much of selling is about how you approach the sale, and really understanding the impact that you are having. Bruce has managed to capture the essence of the best and provides it in an easy to understand clear text that inspires and motivates as you read. Bruce starts with the end in mind, fixes your sales time management and moves onto the other sales blockers we suffer from. Bruce ensures results from day one."

WILLIAM BUIST
Chairman, Abelard Management Services

"A concrete, practical guide to boom your sales creating a value added vision and combining it with smart techniques and tips ready to go. A unique 6 steps book to lift your sales sky high like a rocket!"

PAOLO PETRONIO
GIA Trading Group EU-CIS Managing Director

"As a professional Business Coach, I can assure you that there is no wasted Real Estate in Bruce King's latest book. It not only contains important sales tips and techniques, but it is like having your own personal Coach standing over your shoulder!"

FRANKIE PICASSO — **The Unstoppable Coach,
turning Impossible Goals into Unstoppable Outcomes.**

"Doubling your sales in six weeks sounds like a tall order doesn't it? But this book makes it all possible. Bruce provides you with straightforward, down-to-earth advice and ideas that boost your ability to sell more, rapidly. How do I know? I tried just one of his strategies and it opened up several new opportunities for me within hours. This book is a "must read" if you want to sell more.

GRAHAM JONES
Internet Psychologist

Contents

ABOUT THE AUTHOR

Bruce King is a Fellow of the Institute of Directors, a Member of The Professional Speakers Association, and a Fellow of The Institute of Sales & Marketing Management. As well as being a highly successful salesperson himself, he has also been coaching others to sell for over twenty-five years. During that time he has worked for and coached sales personnel in some of the most successful companies in the world. He addresses audiences internationally on the subjects of sales, inspiration, motivation and becoming World-Class Achievers.

Bruce King's first book—'PSYCHO-SELLING—HOW TO DOUBLE YOUR INCOME FROM SALES IN 8 WEEKS', was first published by BBC Books. It reached number two in 'The Times Best Selling Business Books' chart and was translated into numerous languages. As the title 'HOW TO DOUBLE YOUR SALES IN 6 WEEKS' suggests, he continues to get better as he gets older.

Acknowledgments

There have been so many people who have inspired me over the years and to mention them all would not be possible. The following are those who are closest to me and to whom I want to offer my most grateful thanks.

My parents Sylvia and Eddie. No longer with us in body, but certainly in spirit. They were a shining example of how one can have all the happiness one could ever need, just by being with one another. They also showed me, by example, the importance of never giving up.

My younger brother Graham. Also no longer with us, Graham lived his life just the way he wanted—no compromise! He was an actor and musician and was the first person to give me lessons in public speaking.

My wonderful wife Stephanie. Thank you for standing by me and having faith in me, whatever direction I decided to take in my career and life. Your faith in me is the biggest inspiration I have.

My dearest daughters Gemma and Natasha. I know that I inspired you to understand that you could achieve anything you wanted in life and I am so proud of you both that you did, and continue to do just that. Your successes inspire me too. You are my legacy.

My Grandson Asher—my daughter Gemma's first child. Sitting there with Asher in my arms when he was just a few weeks old, and seeing his eyes dart around the room, time seemed to stand still. In that stillness I came to understand more deeply some of the things I had always known and teach, but with a very different insight, because he was my grandchild.

Aside from what spiritual essence he may have inherited from his parents, and from my wife and I, his grandparents, he was starting with an absolutely clean slate.

This little boy had no history, no previous experiences to cloud his judgement or influence his decisions, no reasons to hold back from exploring his world and building his life. And then I realised that Asher, and indeed every newborn baby, has a lesson for us all, because every day, we too wake up with a clean slate and are starting from scratch all over again. What we do is up to us. Thank you little man!

And last, but certainly not least, thank you Shirley Sharpe, a wonderful lady, a great friend and confidante. Someone who sees so clearly what is beyond.

FOREWORD

The conference presenter finished introducing me with the words "…so please give a warm welcome to Bruce King from England who, in the next five hours, is going to show you how you, too, can double your sales."

I walked slowly across the stage in a blaze of spotlights and to the sound of one thousand delegates clapping. I stood centre stage smiling out at the sea of faces, waiting for the clapping to die down and looking for 'the one'. There is always one in every audience and it rarely takes me more than fifteen seconds to spot them.

'The one' always sits in the first six rows from the stage, near enough to be able to make direct eye contact with me. There is something about their posture and the way they look at me that differentiates them from everyone around them. They almost glow with anticipation and excitement.

'The one' is a person I can be absolutely certain will, as a result of spending a few minutes speaking with me, definitely double their sales in a matter of a few weeks. They will go on to become more successful than they ever dreamed was possible and they will maintain contact with me for the rest of our lives. On this occasion 'the one' was sitting in the third row back and slightly to the left of centre stage. I didn't know it yet but his name was Henry Wall.

At first break, and just as I knew he would, Henry sprung out of his seat and darted towards me as I walked down off the stage. He politely asked if he could grab a coffee with me and ask me a couple of questions.

They are almost always the same two questions. The first is usually "Is How To Double Your Sales In 6 Weeks just a catchy title to sell tickets or does it really work?" The second is "If I really put my mind to it and follow your programme but get stuck once in a while, is it OK for me to e-mail you or telephone for some help and advice". My answers to both questions are always 'yes'.

The first contact I had from Henry was five weeks later. It was an e-mail and simply said "Hey Bruce. Doubled in five. Thanks Buddy! I'll be in touch."

The second contact from Henry was almost a year later. It was another e-mail, this time inviting me to "the best dinner you've ever eaten the next time you are visiting Boston or New York".

I met up with Henry for dinner about three months later. It was certainly one of the best dinners I had ever had, but more so because of the story Henry had to tell me than for the food.

In the previous sixteen months Henry had risen from a junior position in sales where he was earning an average monthly salary plus commission totalling around five thousand dollars to Sales Director, managing a team of seventy eight sales people and earning an average monthly income of around twenty-five thousand dollars. His lifestyle had changed beyond belief; he was living in his dream home, driving his dream car and was utterly convinced that he could go on to achieve anything and everything he wanted in life. Henry put his amazing success down to the fact that he had attended my conference, put everything he learned that day into practice and taught his sales team those same techniques.

The material I am going to present to you in this book is far more detailed and comprehensive than what Henry learned from me in that five hour presentation. You have in your hands all the knowledge you need to be able to double your sales in the next six weeks and go on to achieve anything and everything you want in life. Now it is up to you to be 'the one'.

PREFACE

The top five percent of salespeople are among the highest paid individuals in the world today. Of those top five percent, only a few will have any knowledge of some of the techniques taught in this book. Some may have stumbled on them by accident and will not even be aware that they are using them. Others will have learnt one or two from one of the few brilliant salespeople who are prepared to share some of the secrets of their amazing success.

This book represents a radical deviation from the style and content of most books that claim to improve your sales performance. In the chapters that follow you will learn techniques to take you right to the top of what is one of the oldest, boldest and most lucrative forms of employment available today.

As a former student of psychology, I have always been fascinated by the mental processes involved when people make decisions. When I first embarked on my selling career I set out to investigate and fine tune these processes so that nobody I was trying to sell to would ever say 'no' to me. They very rarely do.

It has taken me years to develop and perfect my techniques and involved me in hundreds of hours of study—and hundreds more practising and perfecting my ideas. However, it is not going to take you that long. The years of practice, and my eagerness to pass this knowledge on to other people, also led me to simplify my ideas so that they could be taught in the shortest possible time and to maximum effect. By following my instructions you are certainly going to be in a position where, within six weeks, you can be selling twice as much as you have ever sold before.

How do I know this? It's quite simple. Thousands of people have already dramatically increased their incomes beyond their wildest dreams as a result of learning these new skills. In some countries where I have presented these ideas through workshops and conferences, much of the audience had a less than perfect understanding of the English language in which I delivered this material. In spite of that, many of them still went on to double their sales.

I taught the 'Power Fist' technique you will find described later to a computer salesman while sharing a cab for fifteen minutes on a wet Thursday afternoon. He called me the following morning to tell me he had signed a contract with his client that had earned him more on that one sale than he had earned in the previous seven months. During our drive he had told me that he felt his chances of closing that sale were one in a thousand. By the time our journey had ended, I knew there was only one chance in a thousand that he would not close it.

I taught the same technique to a group of eight life insurance salespeople in a half-hour session. During the following week, seven of them earned twice as much as in any other week in the previous six months.

A little while ago I received a letter from a saleswoman who had been on one of my weekend training seminars the previous year. At that time she had been unable to meet the sales targets set by her company and was considering leaving her job and going back to college. The letter contained a photograph of her standing beside her brand-new sports car, a gift from the company. Not only had she sold twice as much as the runner-up in the firm's sales competition, she had also been offered a promotion to sales manager. She declined. She was already earning much more than the sales manager's boss.

These are just a few examples of how learning my selling techniques have worked for other people—and how they can work for you. But now let me give you just one example of how psychology can work both for you and against you in sales.

Richard is a top salesman with a large manufacturer of agricultural machinery. He attended my seminar because, in his own words, "I want to be even better than I am now". During one of the breaks he told me how his business had failed, how he had been on the point of giving up on life and how, ten years previously, in a last desperate effort, he had applied for a sales job with an office equipment company.

As with so many people when they are first recruited into the sales profession, his prospective employer had sold him the job. Let's face it, when a company pays a very low salary, if any at all, and when your income is dependent on you getting out there and selling, they don't have a great deal to lose if they make the wrong choice. Richard was told that the job was easy, that he would make a fortune, that anyone could do it and that little training was necessary. He took the job and, after four days learning about the products he was to sell, off he went into the big wide world. All the enthusiasm engendered during those first few days rubbed off on him. Psychology at work. After the first week on the road he returned to the office with a bundle of order forms for various items of equipment. He felt good about himself for the first time in ages. Life was good again—or was it? Back at the office he met some of his sales colleagues and that was when psychology turned against him.

"You've been lucky this week", one said.

"Your first week is always good and after that it's downhill all the way", another said.

"The competition's too stiff", remarked a third.

Guess what? Correct. At the end of the second week he had not sold anything.

Fortunately for Richard, he never forgot the excitement of that first week, or the money he had made. He vowed to make a success of himself. He improved his knowledge of his product range, went to various sales training courses to polish his sales techniques and studied avariciously. He has never looked back. Yet that non-positive encounter with the effects of psychology could have ended his sales career in one week.

Before I go on to explain how to use this book let me emphasise that, although I am going to teach you techniques which will increase your sales dramatically, these are not a substitute for a poor technical knowledge of your product or service. If you don't know enough about what you are trying to sell, you had better find out fast.

I have often heard sales managers tell their salespeople that technical knowledge is not important; that as long as they know five percent more than the person they are selling to they will appear to be experts. Make no mistake about that statement—it is rubbish. If you really want the fortune that being a top salesperson can bring, it is essential to know the technical aspects of the product or service you are selling. Why? First of all, and particularly due to the amount of information freely available on the internet, the average customer is a lot more informed than he or she might have been some years ago. They are looking for expert advice and in this highly competitive world it is readily available to them. If you don't know everything you should know about what you are selling, how can you expect anyone to buy it?

How To Use This Book

"It is a mistake to look too far ahead. Only one
link in the chain of destiny can be handled at a time"
Winston Churchill

Most books on the techniques of selling tend to concentrate almost entirely on prospecting for new customers, presentation skills, handling objections and closing the sale. I have nothing against that approach except that, for most people, it does not work.

I, too, will be covering those same topics in later chapters, in a lot of detail and in ways that you may not have been aware of before now. The difference is, by the time you get to them, the techniques you will have learned to boost your confidence and enthusiasm, for taking control of the selling situation and to enthuse your prospects, will increase the effectiveness of what you will learn several fold.

During your induction into these sales techniques I am also going to ask you to do various things that you may not be used to doing and which, at first, may make you feel a little uncomfortable. To illustrate my point, do the following exercise now:

Put your hands in front of you and interlock your fingers and thumbs.

Now take them apart and, this time, interlock them so that the other thumb is on top.

How does that feel now? Does it feel different? 'Uncomfortable' is how most people describe the feeling when we do this exercise at one of my workshops. But do it often enough and it soon starts to feel comfortable.

I am sure you have heard the expression 'If you carry on doing things the way you have always done them, then the best you are likely to get are the same results'. If you really want to double your sales in the next six weeks, you are going to have to step out of your comfort zone and start doing the things I teach you in order to help you get to where we both want you to be. All I ask is that you give me an hour of your time every day and practice the lessons you will learn. In only six weeks' time, you can be selling twice as much as you have ever sold before—so give us both a chance!

Here is how to use this book. Firstly, study the next chapter titled 'Programming Your Mind To Double Your Sales'. You will be taught some simple mental exercises, which you need to do EVERY DAY FOR AT LEAST THE NEXT SIX WEEKS, together with some other straightforward and essential activities. These exercises will take up only approximately half an hour, every day, and are crucial to your success. When you experience how powerful these techniques are you will no doubt want to carry on using them long after the six weeks is up, not only to double your sales but to achieve anything else you may want in life.

The chapter after that deals with some psychological barriers to success; not only to success in sales but in every area of your life. If you are suffering from any of the syndromes I describe, that is the time to deal with them once and for ever.

From then on we will focus on the practical techniques you need to learn in order for you to double your sales. I want you to study only one chapter a week. Read that chapter several times during that week and incorporate everything I teach you into your normal working day. In other words, don't just read it - do it! Do not attempt to go ahead to another chapter before the week is out. Real learning can only take place and habits can only be changed a small step at a time. What you learn needs to be practised and reinforced before moving on. Let's face it - six weeks to Double Your Sales is hardly a long time to wait, so please keep to this format, which I know will work for you.

Chapter One

Programming Your Mind

To Double Your Sales

"Whatever the mind can conceive and believe, the mind can achieve"
Napoleon Hill, *Author of Think and Grow Rich*

How The Human Brain Works

One of the first things you have to do in order to double your sales in six weeks, or indeed achieve anything you want in life very quickly, is to train your brain to believe you can, and to train it to help you to achieve that. So let us first of all take a look at how the human brain works.

The human brain is incredibly complicated. It's made up of at least one hundred billion neurones which is the technical name for nerve cells. To get that into perspective, imagine a one kilogram bag of fine, granulated sugar. It contains approximately three million granules. If there are one hundred billion nerve cells in the brain, we would need thirty one thousand bags of sugar to represent that quantity.

Recent research has uncovered remarkable new findings about the impact of experience on the brain. We know that every experience triggers neuronal development within the brain which means that the more areas of the brain which are stimulated and used, the more neuronal pathways and networks are established. As we live our lives our experience gradually remoulds us. Connections are made in the brain and connections are broken. We learn and we forget. Experience shapes the way our brains operate and after a few repetitions of an experience, cell groups working together team up and become much more powerful.

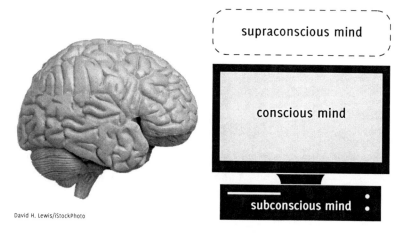

David H. Lewis/iStockPhoto

Again, for the sake of simplicity, I like to compare the human brain to a computer. (See illustration). Firstly we have the conscious mind. I liken that to the screen on your computer. It is what you are conscious of at any given time. It is the words and sounds you are conscious of hearing and the words you say to yourself when you are thinking. It is what you are looking at and the pictures you create in your mind when you are thinking and when other people are speaking to you. The conscious mind is what you are aware of.

Then we have the subconscious mind, which I liken to the hard drive on your computer. Everything that ever appears on your computer screen or in the conscious mind is stored in the subconscious mind, or hard drive. Everything from the day you were born. Some experts say that this even happens whilst you are still in your mother's womb. The only difference between your brain and the computer is that you do not need to press a 'save' button for it to be stored; it happens automatically and is out of your control.

Day by day, month by month and year by year, everything you experience in your conscious mind is stored in your subconscious mind and, over time, we build up automatic connections between the conscious and the subconscious mind. Scientists call these neuronal pathways. In this way, whenever your conscious mind perceives anything, it automatically links to a previous experience stored in your subconscious mind that relates to that particular item of information. According to Professor Chris Frith, one of the world's most renowned experts on the human brain, "free will is illusory in that before we consciously decide to do anything, our subconscious mind has already made the decision on what we are going to do". In fact 99.999% of everything we do and think, happens on a subconscious level. In other words—we are all programmed rather like robots!

The major ways in which we create these neuronal pathways, or automatic links, are through the words we hear and the words we say, through the pictures we see around us and the pictures we create in our minds, the combination of which create feelings. The problem we have is that, according to behavioural psychologists, for every one positive experience, we have forty-eight negative experiences. In other words, we are programmed to fail. I will illustrate this with a few examples:

There is very little good news in the newspapers and on television. Good news doesn't sell, so we are constantly bombarded with negative, or what I prefer to call 'non-positive' messages, which are stored in the subconscious mind.

Did you ever have the words 'must try harder' written on any of your school reports? If you did, then you associate the word 'try' with failure. So later in life when somebody says they will 'try' and do something for you, you don't really expect them to do it. Neither does your subconscious mind help you when you say you will try and do something. Most times you do not.

Do you feel a little uncomfortable cold calling or talking to strangers when you are networking? If you do, there's a good chance that is because your parents told you 'not to talk to strangers' when you were a child.

Have you ever experienced a 'strong gut feeling' about any situation? Of course you have. That is the subconscious mind sending you a message.

There is one more part to the brain that you need to be aware of—the supraconscious mind. I liken this to the radiation coming off your computer. More on the supraconscious mind follows later in this chapter.

Let us take a closer look at how negative messages can affect your subconscious mind, your mental state and sales performance.

When you first picked up this book you may have thought that it wasn't really possible to double your sales in six weeks, but if you could just get a ten to fifteen percent increase in sales you would be happy. If so, what you did was simply programme your subconscious mind to restrict your increase in sales to ten to fifteen percent.

You may have thought that you would nevertheless 'try' to double your sales. We have already mentioned the word 'try' and its' negative connotation. If you try to double your sales, you will almost certainly fail to do so.

When somebody telephones you and says "I'm sorry to bother you but…", how do you feel? It is likely you will be less than enthusiastic to have a conversation with them. The words 'I'm sorry' connect to experiences in your subconscious mind when somebody had done something wrong. The word 'bother' is subconsciously associated with somebody being a nuisance. Then they say 'but', which means in spite of the fact that they know they are doing something wrong and are going to be a nuisance, they are going to do it anyway! Do you use that expression sometimes?

How many times have you heard or said the words 'no problem' when somebody has requested something. Think about the word 'problem' and what it could be associated with in somebody's subconscious mind.

How about "don't hesitate to call me"? What is the word 'hesitate' going to connect to or implant in the subconscious mind? Hesitation of course!

Have you ever said to anyone, "would you object to me calling you tomorrow?" When you ask that, they automatically have a subconscious 'objection' to what you have suggested. So the words you speak and the words you hear can have a dramatic and non-positive effect on your and other people's subconscious mind.

How about the pictures we see around us and the pictures we create in our minds when we are thinking about something? The following is a demonstration I have carried out hundreds of times on stage at conferences around the world. You can do this at home now, although you need somebody to help you with this.

Stand up straight and hold your strongest arm straight out in front of you with the palm of your hand facing down. Ask the person helping you to put their hand over your extended wrist and press down very firmly. At the same time you must resist their downward pressure on your arm with all your strength. Just one word of caution—this is not a competition to see who is strongest. You are just working together to see how strong your arm feels. When you do this, you'll be able to resist the downward pressure quite easily.

Now repeat the exercise but this time whilst you are looking at the picture below. This is a cartoon of a salesperson whose sales have fallen dramatically and they do not know what to do about it. I call him 'Mr Negative'.

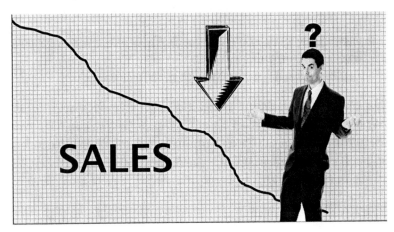

I guarantee your arm was a lot weaker this time! The negative picture you were looking at connected with other negative situations in your subconscious mind and your body became weaker as a result. The negative or non-positive pictures we see around us and in our minds can have an extraordinarily powerful non-positive effect on our entire state. As I said previously, words and pictures create feelings and if we hear non-positive words or see non-positive pictures, we feel non-positive at a subconscious level, which of course affects our conscious mind too.

PSYCHO-DYNAMIC PROGRAMMING (PDP)

In this section I am going to teach you several techniques and exercises that will help you to programme your subconscious mind to enable you to double your sales in the next six weeks. I call these techniques Psycho-Dynamic Programming. Now let's not confuse these techniques with brainwashing. Brainwashing is something that is forced upon you but by investing in this book you volunteered to double your sales. Having said that, I can think of a lot of good reasons for people having their brains washed out once in a while to get rid of some of those cobwebs that have been holding them back from the success they deserve.

A Few Words on Goal Setting

I am sure you know how important goal setting is. Some expressions that spring to mind are:

- If you don't know where you are going, how will you ever know when you get there?
- A person without goals is like a ship without a rudder

One of the most powerful things that someone once said to me and had the biggest impact on my life was: "Bruce, you have two choices in life: You can be an extra in somebody else's production or the star of your own. Without clearly defined goals you'll just be someone else's extra!"

From the point of view of what we are doing together, there is only one goal! I want you to double your sales and you presumably want to also. Enough said!

24

PDP TECHNIQUES

When the subconscious mind has a totally clear picture of what you want to achieve, it goes on autopilot to help you attain those goals. In order to get it into autopilot mode, the subconscious mind needs constant reminders in various ways of the goal you have set out to achieve. Use the following three techniques every day, and after just seven days I guarantee you will start to see some quite extraordinary changes in your attitude, your energy levels, your confidence and, of course, your sales.

Now here is the most important point for you to understand. I told you earlier that our brains were a little like computers and that you were programmed rather like a robot. So here is the key point...

You do not need to believe these techniques for them to work. They will—whether you believe it or not! You just have to use them.

PDP Technique 1 - Post Your Goal to Double Your Sales

Purchase a pad of yellow adhesive notes and write on them as in the following illustration.

Write your name in the space indicated and put in a date by which you want to achieve this goal. The date is very important because a goal without a deadline is nothing more than a dream, or possibly even a delusion. Goals must have a specific deadline in order to be achieved.

I (your name) will double my sales by (date)

Write out about twenty-five of these notes and place them where you will come across them frequently during the course of the day. For example: on the corner of your computer screen, on the wall by your desk, on the dashboard or windscreen of your car, on your bathroom mirror, on the refrigerator door and anywhere else where you will see them often. You do not have to read the words every time you see them. Your subconscious mind will automatically recognise the words and continuously reinforce that message. You will be programming your subconscious mind to double your sales by that date.

PDP Technique 2 – Affirm Your Goal to Double Your Sales

In order to programme your subconscious mind to double your sales it also needs to hear what you want to achieve. Therefore the next technique is to create and use a 'power affirmation'.

An affirmation is a scientifically proven form of auto-suggestion. It is a statement that you repeat over and over to yourself and is a promise to yourself that you will achieve a specific objective. In this case the objective is to double your sales and this is the paragraph I want you to write down and learn:

> *'I (your name) am committed to doubling my sales by (date) and they are already increasing rapidly. Nothing will stand in the way of me making (£X) in personal income this year.'*

Insert your name and the date you intend to have doubled your sales by. Calculate the income you will make when you have doubled your sales and insert that figure.

- Learn the affirmation off by heart
- Say it aloud and with feeling at least 15 times, three times a day

You can do this in the car, in the lift, whilst having a shower, walking in the park, jogging and any other time it is convenient for you to do so. The more times you say it every day, the faster you will programme your subconscious mind to help you achieve your goal to double your sales.

PDP Technique 3 – Visualise Your Goal to Double Your Sales

This PDP technique is, without question, the most powerful of them all. Some years ago I was involved in teaching people to walk barefoot across beds of burning hot coals. The reason for these 'Fire-Walking Seminars' was to demonstrate that it is possible to achieve the seemingly impossible in a very short period of time. The training consisted of a short period of relaxation, followed by twenty minutes of visualising walking across the red hot coals. More than fifty people were taught this simple visualisation technique at each one of our seminars and at the end of the training very few lacked the confidence to walk across the burning coals. With few exceptions, there was not a blister in sight. Visualisation is the key to programming the subconscious mind, and one of the keys to helping you double your sales. Because it is so important, I am going to explain in more detail why this is such a powerful technique.

When you put an absolutely clear picture into your subconscious mind there are two main effects. Firstly, the effect this has on you and secondly, the effect it has on others.

THE EFFECT VISUALISATION HAS ON *YOU*

The first effect visualisation will have on you is based on the fact that the brain cannot tell the difference between imagination and reality. Here are a few examples to illustrate this.

In a moment, I want you to close your eyes and picture a lemon on a chopping board. Then see yourself cutting the lemon in half with a very sharp knife, revealing the shiny inside of the lemon and seeing the juice running down the side of the knife blade. Then picture yourself cutting a thin slice of the lemon, putting it inside your mouth and sucking it. Do that now.

Did you experience a strange feeling in your mouth just as you would have if you had actually been sucking on a piece of lemon? I'm sure you did experience that sensation—but you were only imagining the lemon. The mind simply cannot tell the difference between imagination and reality.

Major James Nesbeth spent seven years as a prisoner of war in Vietnam. During those seven years he was imprisoned in a cage that measured only four and one-half feet high by four feet wide and four feet long. Throughout almost the entire time he was a prisoner he saw no one, talked to no one and had no physical activity. In order to keep his sanity and his mind active, he described how he used visualisation techniques.

Every day, in his mind, he would play a game of golf—a full eighteen-hole game at his favourite golf course. In his mind, he would create pictures of the trees on the course, he would see and smell the freshly mown grass, hear and feel the wind and hear the songs of the birds. He created different weather conditions—windy spring days, overcast winter days and sunny summer mornings. He felt the grip of the club in his hands as he played his shots in his mind. He watched the ball arc down the fairway and land at the exact spot he had selected. He did this in his mind, seven days a week for seven years. He took as long playing this round of golf in his mind as if he were actually playing the course.

When Major Nesbeth was finally released and had the opportunity to play his first round of golf on that favourite golf course, he found that he had cut twenty strokes off his golfing average without having touched a golf club in seven years—just by practicing in his mind. A further example demonstrating that the mind cannot tell the difference between imagination and reality.

There was an experiment carried out with a group of basketball players in the USA. Thirty professional players were brought in and tested on their ability to take penalty shots. Once their standards were assessed they were split into three groups of ten. The first group was sent home and told to just rest up and forget about basketball for a week. The second group was brought in daily for seven days and made to practice taking penalty shots for one hour a day. The third group was instructed to stay at home, practice taking penalty shots in their mind and to see themselves getting a one hundred percent score rate.

At the end of the week the three groups were brought back in and re-tested. The group that had done nothing remained at the same standard. The group that had come back and physically practiced every day improved their performance by five percent. The group that had practiced in their minds every day improved by a staggering fourteen percent. Again, illustrating that the mind cannot tell the difference between imagination and reality.

The second effect visualisation has on you is that it trains your subconscious mind to become a 'Goal Magnet'. Another way to put this is to say that what you focus on is what you attract.

Human beings are constantly bombarded with sounds and pictures. If you tried to consciously focus on every sound and picture that was available to you, your brain simply could not take in all the information. So the brain sorts information related to what we are focusing on at the time.

To illustrate the point, without moving your head or your eyes, look at everything else you can possibly see right now aside from the words you are reading.

You have probably noticed lots of things that you were not seeing before I asked you to do this, even though they were in your field of vision. You were just seeing what was important to you at the time. Your brain filtered out what was not relevant to the task in hand. In the same way, when we have a totally clear picture in our minds as to what we want to achieve, our brains filter out everything that is not relevant to those goals and just highlights for us the things we need to see and do in order to achieve them.

THE EFFECT VISUALISATION HAS ON OTHERS

When I first start to discuss this topic at my conferences and workshops, approximately fifty percent of the audience think I may be in need of seeing a psychiatrist. By the time I have finished, half of them may be converted and the remainder will never accept what I am about to tell you. I can, however, assure you that there is a large body of scientific evidence to support these theories, but we do not have the scope within this book to give you a grounding in quantum physics and the associated subjects that underpin them. So I shall keep it simple.

I, and millions of other people around the world, are convinced that every human being is in some way connected to every other human being by an invisible network. An analogy could be the internet. I have been studying this subject for many years and one of the scientists whose work I have been following closely is Doctor Rupert Sheldrake, an Englishman with a PhD in Biology, and possibly one of the most respected, albeit controversial, scientists in the world.

According to Doctor Sheldrake we are all connected and operate within living fields of thought and perception. These fields, says Sheldrake, are non-material fields of influence—invisible forces that structure space and behaviour. He uses gravity as one example in that we cannot see it, it is not a material object, but it is certainly real. Gravity gives things weight and makes things full. He says there are measurable magnetic fields that underlie the functioning of every part of our body and countless vibratory patterns of activity occur within these fields which we cannot detect with any of our five senses, although we sometimes 'sense' them.

Doctor Sheldrake also says that there are quantum matter fields which scientists say are the real substance of the universe—states of space full of energy and invisible structures that interconnect. I may be losing you now so here are a few of the examples he uses to illustrate his views.

A carrot seed grows into the shape of a carrot because it is directed to by the cumulative energy fields of all previous carrots.

A million blind African termites build a ten foot tall nest, featuring top-to-bottom ventilation shafts and other complex architectures, because they are guided by the cumulative energy fields of previous termite nests.

A dog anticipates its owner's return and dogs and cats find owners who have moved hundreds of miles away because the bond they forge through close association is an energy field which can be traced.

A newspaper crossword puzzle is easier to solve late in the day, because the energy of the correct answers broadcast by thousands of successful solvers facilitates the task.

Now take just two examples which you can probably relate to a lot more easily and which may help to convince you of this concept.

You have been driving along in your car, in that way we sometimes

30

do, where we are almost on autopilot, or you have been sitting quietly in your office with your mind drifting. Suddenly somebody's face or name just pops into your mind. Have you ever, within a short while of that happening, received a telephone call from that very person and said "That's funny—I was just thinking about you", or you telephone them and they say the same thing? I know you have.

When I ask an audience of a thousand people that question, almost every hand goes up. Then I then ask them if it has happened several times and every hand goes up again. This is not coincidence. This is you, or they, communicating thoughts and attracting people through these energy fields.

A little while ago I received a letter from a life insurance salesman. He wrote the following:

Dear Bruce,

I attended your workshop on selling last month. I did think the exercise on visualisation was a bit off the wall, to put it politely. But as so much of what else you taught us made so much sense, I thought I would give it a try anyway.

Life insurance is very hard to sell unless it's associated with a mortgage and, in my eleven years in the business, I have never had anyone volunteer to buy some life insurance. So to test your theory I visualised somebody calling me whom I had never met before and asking to buy some life insurance.

I am totally flabbergasted. On the fourth day I had two people call me who asked for just that! I am a convert—watch this space!

Sincerely,

Richard Montgomery

The fact is that we are all connected in some way and any thought by any human can be transmitted to anyone else in the species. The stronger the thought and the deeper in the subconscious—the stronger the energy's resonance and the more likely other people who can help you to achieve your goals are going to be attracted to you—the mind magnet!

Now it should be quite obvious that if we were to walk around all day long totally focused on visualising ourselves achieving our goals, we would never achieve anything. So instead of having the picture in our conscious mind, we have to put it deep and powerfully into our subconscious mind. Here is what you do to achieve that.

Do this exercise every day, twice a day:

Find a quiet place where you are not going to be disturbed for twenty minutes. This could be a room in your home, a spare office at your place of work, or your car. I love carrying out these exercises in my car because I feel it is a very private space, almost like a cocoon, and I can park up anywhere where it is quiet, turn off my mobile telephone and know I will not be disturbed.

Now I want you to close your eyes and, for just three minutes, relax and focus on breathing gently and listening to and feeling the breath going in and out of your body. You should feel very relaxed by the end of those three minutes.

Next, and for the following seventeen minutes, I want you to visualise in as much detail as possible precisely how your life would be if you had already achieved your goal of doubling your sales. I want you to see the pictures you associate with having doubled your sales. Those pictures might be you sitting in a much more prestigious car, or a larger office, seeing your bank statement with a very healthy balance on it, living in a new home, or sitting on a beach in Barbados. Whatever the pictures are that you associate with doubling your sales—see those pictures clearly and in the greatest of detail.

If, for example, you want to own a new sports car, you need to know the make, the colour of the paintwork and upholstery, the look of the dashboard, the colour and finish on the steering-wheel and the make of tyre. In other words, everything that would enable a stranger to produce a detailed picture of what is in your mind must be visualised.

32

If it is a new house, the same applies. You need to visualise the colour of the brickwork, the window-frames and the roof. You need to visualise the number of rooms and the décor in every one of those rooms, right down to the last detail. Most important, you need to visualise yourself living there, just as you need to imagine yourself owning and driving the sports car.

I also want you to hear the sounds associated with those pictures. It could be the sound of the exhaust or the engine of your new, prestige car. It could be the sound of people clapping and congratulating you on your large bonus and promotion. It could be the sound of the waves lapping the beach in Barbados. Whatever the sounds are that are associated with those pictures I want you to hear them.

Lastly, I want you to get in touch with your feelings. I want you to feel as you would feel if you had doubled your sales and were experiencing everything that went with that.

Any and every time you are doing this visualisation exercise and you feel at your very best, most excited and powerful, clench your fist and hold it against your body on a spot just below your navel. I call this the 'Power Fist' technique. Whenever you want to experience that exciting and powerful feeling again at any time during the day, simply clench your fist and hold it in that same spot and you will automatically get in touch with those same powerful feelings. Your Power Fist can carry you through some of the more difficult challenges you may face during the course of your working day with the greatest of ease. The Power Fist gives you all the power you could ever need, whenever you need it.

The first few times you carry out this exercise you may find that your mind tends to drift a little and you start thinking about other things. That is perfectly normal and nothing to be concerned about. As soon as you notice you have done this, just go back to the exercise. There is no need to make up for the time you lost when your mind drifted.

Your responsibility is to carry out these three PDP exercises every single day for at least the next six weeks. Most people tell me that they start to see quite extraordinary results within just a few days. There are a few more things I want you to do every day for the next six weeks to ensure you achieve your goal to Double Your Sales.

1: Keep A Goal Book

Buy a smart leather or vinyl bound book with numerous blank sheets into which you can paste pictures. Write your Power Affirmation on the first page in large, bold letters. Over the next few weeks collect and paste in pictures of the things you associate with having already achieved your goals. These could be pictures of your new car, your new office, your new house or your holiday in Barbados. Whatever pictures you come across that excite you and represent what you would be doing when you have doubled your sales, cut them out and paste them in. Keep your Goal Book with you at all times and look through it at least once a day.

Some of the people who have attended my workshops put a great deal of their success down to keeping a Goal Book. Some have even said it was the most important factor in helping them to double their sales.

2: Keep A Journal

Buy a large diary with plenty of space for each day, which is for the purpose of keeping a journal. At the end of every day, spend just five minutes writing down all the good things that have happened to you that day. They do not have to be monumental achievements – just the good things that have happened to you that you believe are helping you move towards your goal of doubling your sales.

Also write down the things you have thought about that day, ideas that have 'popped into your mind' that you believe will also help you to achieve your goal of doubling your sales. When you have finished doing those written exercises, read what you have written and congratulate yourself for your achievements to date and on what you are going to do in the future.

3: Change The Words You Use

From now on, I want you to be particularly conscious of the words you use when speaking to other people and the words you use in your mind when talking to yourself, and to change any non-positive words and phrases you use into positive ones. For example:

Instead of: It's not possible
Say: It is possible

Instead of: I'll try
Say: I will

Instead of: I'm sorry to bother you but...
Say: I have something to run past you which I'm sure you will be very excited about. Is now a good time to speak or shall I call you back a little later?

Instead of: No problem
Say: It's a pleasure

Instead of: Would you object if I called you tomorrow?
Say: May I call you tomorrow please?

Listen very carefully to what you are saying to other people and, if you hear yourself saying anything with a non-positive connotation, correct yourself on the spot. Say something like—'let me re-phrase that'. When you are talking to yourself, do the same. From now on, it's time to start communicating with others and yourself in a totally positive way.

The following amusing story illustrates how non-positive thinking can create a non-positive result:

Mr Jones, a farmer, needed to plough his field before the dry spell set in, but his own plough had broken. "I know, I'll ask my neighbour, farmer Smith, if I can borrow his plough. He's a good man; I'm sure he'll have done his ploughing by now and he'll be glad to lend me his machine." So Mr Jones began to walk the four fields to Smith's farm.

After a field of walking, farmer Jones said to himself, "I hope that farmer Smith has finished all his own ploughing or he'll not be able to lend me his machine."

Then after a few more minutes of worrying and walking, farmer Jones said to himself, "What if Smith's plough is old and on its' last legs—he'll never be wanting to lend it to me will he?"

After another field, farmer Jones said to himself, "Farmer Smith was never a very helpful fellow, I reckon maybe he won't be too keen to lend me his plough even if it's in perfect working order and he's finished all his own ploughing weeks ago."

As farmer Jones arrives at farmer Smith's farm, farmer Jones is thinking to himself: "That old Smith can be a mean old fellow. I reckon even if he's got all his ploughing done, and his own machine is sitting there doing nothing, he'll not lend it to me just so he can watch me go to ruin."

Farmer Jones then walked up farmer Smith's front path, knocked on the door, and farmer Smith answered. "Well good morning Jones, what can I do for you?" said farmer Smith. Farmer Jones, with eyes bulging and a red face said, "Mr Smith, you can take your bloody plough, and you can stick it up your back side!"

4: Avoid Energy Vampires

You are surrounded by non-positive people who are capable of sapping your positive energy. They will tell you that your goals to double your sales are crazy and impossible to achieve. They may laugh at your vision for success and be intent on bringing you down to their level. Do not let this happen. You will not be the first person to have doubled your sales using these techniques; thousands have gone before you.

If you had already achieved your goal of doubling your sales and living the lifestyle you want and deserve, would you be spending time with these people? Would you be mixing in a different business and social circle? I hope not. The time to make these changes is NOW. Act as if you are already the success you intend to be. Jim Rohn, the hugely successful author and self-made millionaire, put it most powerfully when he said: "You are the average of the five people you spend the most time with!".

5: Change Your Employment Status

If you are already running your own business then this does not apply to you. If you are employed it most certainly does. From now onwards I want you to think of yourself in a different way. Instead of being an employee, I want you to think of yourself as the Chief Executive Officer of your own one-person corporation, currently selling your services to a particular person or company. That is the reality of your situation, so from now on act and behave like that CEO.

ACTION POINTS

Post your goal to Double Your Sales (PDP1)

Affirm your goal to Double Your Sales at least fifteen times, three times daily, for at least the next six weeks (PDP2)

Visualise your goal to Double Your Sales, twice daily for twenty minutes, for at least the next six weeks (PDP3)

Keep a goal book

Keep a daily journal

Change the words you use

Avoid energy vampires

Change your employment status

Chapter Two

Psychological Barriers To Success

"I have lived a long life and had many
troubles, most of which never happened."
Mark Twain

THE POWER OF FEAR

There are several psychological barriers to success which we are going to discuss in this chapter and if you are being held back by any of these, then it is time to change.

Change is going on in the world all the time and so much of this change is out of our control. Most times we either have no choice but to go along with it and accept it. For example, there are cyclical changes in the stock market, changes in the weather in summer and winter, and changes in the value of house prices.

Then there are technological changes, such as the invention of the computer and the mobile telephone, to name but a few. You can choose to go along with these changes or reject them, but inevitably you will almost always accept them. I remember when computers first came out and my secretary swore she would never use one of those "new fangled things". She really did hang on in there but when we could no longer purchase typewriter ribbons she finally gave in and embraced the technology. I also remember when mobile telephones were first introduced and I was adamant I would never have one. Now of course I cannot do without it. I am currently resisting the change to a 'blackberry'.

When it comes to changing yourself and your behaviours for the better, which is something entirely within your control, why then would you even think of resisting it? The answer is probably because you are scared—it is fear! Fear is the one feeling above all other emotions that holds people back from achieving the success they want and deserve and something you need to overcome if you are going to double your sales.

Are you fearful?

Some years ago, when I was working full time in sales, I was driving past a large office block which had the name 'Rogers & Associates — Accountants' on the face of the building in large letters. At the time, I was selling accounting systems for accountants and my first reaction was to stop and call in to introduce myself. Then fear set in. The little voice in my head was recalling past times when I had dropped in without an appointment and had been rejected, or had the opportunity to show them what I was selling and was told it was of no interest. I imagined how it would all be a waste of time. As a result of those thoughts, I kept driving. However, after a few hundred yards I put the brake on my thoughts, turned the car around, drove back and dropped in. It transpired that the senior partner was an old college friend of mine. We had coffee, caught up on old times and, to cut a long story short, a few weeks later I received an order that earned me over four thousand pounds in commission.

The truth of the matter is that most of the things we fear are just in our imagination. According to some psychologists 'fear' stands for FANTASISED EXPERIENCES APPEARING REAL. In other words, the experiences we imagine may happen or they may not happen, but by imaging that they will, we create fear. If you don't believe me, take out half an hour and list as many situations as you can think of when you were scared of what might happen if you did something—but you did it just the same. Then place a tick against those situations where what you feared would happen, did happen. I'm betting there are going to be very few ticks!

Our stone age ancestors used fear as a way of dealing with dangerous situations. It was part of the 'fight or flight' mechanism that helped to keep them safe and the fear created an adrenaline rush that enabled them to deal with the danger. Nowadays, we do not have to deal with the dangers that our ancestors experienced. Today fear is a signal to us that we must be cautious, alert and ready to deal with a specific situation, and we experience the same or a similar adrenaline rush. However, because we do not have to fight or fly, we transfer our fear into situations where we really need not be fearful at all. In spite of that, it is almost guaranteed you are going to experience fear frequently in your life. It is how you face up to it and how you deal with it that will make the difference between failure and success.

To help you understand how you manifest fear, look at the following statements.

- I am afraid of making a cold call.
- I am afraid of the sales presentation I have to make to a group of Directors.
- I am afraid of speaking with the Managing Director.

Now let us re-state each of those in a different way.

- I want to be successful at cold calling but I get fearful by imagining I will be rejected and how I would feel.
- I want to make a good sales presentation to a group of Directors but I get fearful by imagining I will fail to make a good impression.
- I want to speak with the Managing Director but I am fearful because I imagine he will not take me seriously as he is such a higher authority than I.

Do you see how you create the fear by imagining a non-positive outcome? Now ask yourself these questions.

Why should I fear rejection?

Rejection is nothing more than a myth because rejection never leaves me any worse off than before I was rejected.

Why should I fear failure?

It is perfectly OK to fail. As convenient as it might be, I cannot always learn from other people's mistakes. Sometimes I have to fail in order to learn how to do something better.

Why should I fear higher authority figures?

They are just people like me with their own families, their own goals, their own fears and, very often, are very fearful of salespeople too. As for fear of losing a sale; I have never yet met a salesperson who sold to every single person they ever wanted to sell to.

How we deal with fear is a choice

Sometimes we choose to face fear head on and we are exhilarated by it and love the experience. Other times we allow it to freeze us into inactivity.

Did you ever go on one of those real scary roller coaster rides? You were possibly petrified when you were queuing for the ride—but you went anyway!

Do you snow ski? Do you ever get scared when approaching a new and slightly more dangerous run than you are used to? I know you do and I know that most times, if not always, you choose to ski it anyway. How you deal with fear is a choice. So why not always choose to be excited and exhilarated by it? Here is a technique you can use that will enable you to overcome fear and take positive action.

PDP FEAR TECHNIQUE

There will be many times in your life when you overcame a really powerful fear. It could have been the rollercoaster or skiing example I just mentioned. It could have been when you were learning to ride a two wheeled bicycle and your parents took off the rear wheel stabilisers for the first time and said they would push you to get you started. You were possibly petrified and even fell off a few times. Every time you fell off, the fear became worse. Then finally you managed to keep your balance and pedalled off on your own. I know how fantastic you felt afterwards because the same thing happened to me.

Maybe it was the first time you jumped from a diving board into a swimming pool. You may have stood on the top board, looked down, and felt like you were about to leap off the top of a skyscraper.

Despite that, eventually, because you could not lose face in front of your friends or parents, you did it anyway. When you splashed into the water and surfaced, I know you felt amazing.

Could it have been the first time you made a sales presentation to a board of Directors and walked away with the sale? Did you leave the office building, and once you were round the first corner, leap into the air and shout for joy?

Whatever that experience was when you overcame a powerful fear, I want you to sit quietly in a chair and replay the whole scene through in your mind. See yourself doing what you did, hear the sounds associated with that experience, and feel all the power and excitement you felt when you beat it. At the moment you are feeling that power and excitement at its highest level, squeeze the lobe of your right ear between your finger and thumb for a few seconds.

Repeat this exercise several times and you will lock that feeling into your subconscious mind and associate it with squeezing your earlobe. Then, whenever you feel fear, squeeze your right earlobe and you will experience all the power and excitement you need to overcome that fear.

Fear is not something to be feared; it can be your greatest ally. Fear is a natural reaction and not something you should feel at all ashamed of admitting. Accept that being fearful is a natural stage in the process of achieving great success. Face the fear with courage and know that eventually, if you do this, you cannot fail to reach your goal of doubling your sales.

I'LL BE HAPPY WHEN...

If you are not happy right now, then it is very unlikely you are going to be happy when you have doubled your sales, and you are not going to be happy while you are on your way to achieving that goal. Unhappy people tend to be non-positive, less inclined to action and often see the worst in every situation rather than the best. Unhappy people also tend to use the expression 'I need' rather than 'I want'. It's great to want more, but it is not OK to need more.

Don't be needy! The word 'needy' is non-positive.

Unhappy people also attract other unhappy people to them, and the unhappy people you attract are going to be less likely to buy than happy ones. If you really want to double your sales, then I suggest you get happy right now. You already have many reasons to be so. For example, you may want a nicer home, but you do have a roof over your head right now and many people do not. You may want a more prestigious car, but you do have the four wheels you need to get around to see all those customers you are going to be selling to. You may want to be able to afford much more expensive designer clothes, but I am assuming you have some nice smart ones anyway. Are you getting the picture now?

If you are not really happy, here is an exercise that I would like you to do right now or at the earliest opportunity. It is one that I have people carry out in my personal development workshops and it can really make you feel a lot happier than you have been for a very long time.

Take a large sheet of paper and write across the top of the page: REASONS FOR ME TO BE HAPPY RIGHT NOW. Take a close look at every area of your life; your work, your relationships, your home, your hobbies and everything else that comes to mind. Make a long list of everything you have got to be happy about in each of these areas. At the end of this long list you should write 'I'm also happy because I am now on my way to doubling my sales!'

When you have finished that list, read it again and then place it in a plastic folder and keep it with you, adding to it as you identify other things that make you happy. Any time you don't feel happy, take it out and read it again.

There's another advantage to being happy; happy people tend to smile a lot. People like people who smile—and people buy from people they like.

IT'S NOT MY FAULT!

Do you make excuses for not achieving? Do you blame other people? Do you complain? If you do, it is time to stop right now. These habits create a motivational deficiency disorder. Everything you are experiencing in your life and work today are the result of choices YOU made in the past and it is time to start taking total responsibility for your life. Let us take these habits one at a time.

Do you make excuses?

If you do then it is going to be a lot harder for you to double your sales, or indeed achieve anything else you want in life. Excuses are a waste of time because no matter how many excuses you make, it will not change you and your situation at all. All it will do is create more non-positive neural pathways into your subconscious mind.

From now on you have to adopt the attitude 'If it is to be, it is up to me!' You have to come from a standpoint that you have always had the power to make a difference in your life but, until now, you have chosen not to use that power. It really does not matter if you chose not to in the past because the past is history and the only people who make money out of history are historians and archaeologists. It is time to change, stop making excuses and take total responsibility for your life. You can take as long over making this decision as you wish. You can think about it and drag it out over the next few weeks, or you can make the decision to take that responsibility right now. Your call!

In the future, when things don't go as well for you as you would have liked, and rest assured things will go wrong, instead of making excuses, ask yourself questions like:

- How did I create that situation?
- What did I say or not say that caused that non-positive result?
- What did I do to get that response?
- How can I make sure that does not happen in the future?
- What do I have to do differently to get the results I want?

Make it a lifelong mission to learn from your mistakes and from your successes and enjoy the experience.

Do you blame other people?

If you are going to double your sales, then you have to stop blaming other people for your lack of sales success. Blame is a waste of time because no matter how much you blame another person, it will not change you and your situation at all. Just like excuses, all it will do is create more non-positive neural pathways into your subconscious mind.

If something goes wrong, accept the blame and ask yourself the same questions to ensure it does not happen again. Of course there will be times when other people involved in the sales process or in the organisation make a mistake and, as a result, sabotage the sale. But, ultimately, people buy from people and it is up to you to overcome the situation. Nothing is insurmountable.

STOP COMPLAINING!

There are two aspects to complaining. The first is complaining about our current situation—and we can only do this when we know that something better already exists. Statements like "I don't have a big enough house", "I don't have a smart enough car", "I'm not earning enough money" or "My sales manager is horrible to me", are all complaints that you can do something about but have taken the decision not to. With this aspect of complaining, you simply need to stop and take total responsibility for your life.

There are also situations where you could have a legitimate complaint about something that is affecting your ability to double your sales as quickly as you wish, or could have resulted in you losing a sale through no fault of your own. Maybe the switchboard operator did not pass an important customer call on to you? Perhaps the order was not delivered on time? Maybe they sent the wrong size or the wrong colour? Things out of your control can and do go wrong and need dealing with, but in the correct manner.

Have you ever noticed that so many people who complain do so to the wrong people? A husband has an issue with his wife but complains to his colleagues at work about her. A mother has an issue with her children but complains to her husband. An employee has an issue with their boss but they complain to their friends or workmates. Why do they do this? The answer is very simple. They complain to others because it is easier than complaining to the person they have the issue with. Of course, that rarely ever resolves the issue.

If you feel you have a reason to complain about something that is affecting your ability to double your sales, you need to deal with the issue with the person who caused the problem—but do not complain. The moment you tell someone you need to complain about something, or you act in a manner that is identified with complaining, their subconscious mind will switch them into a defensive mode and you will not get the level of cooperation you want in dealing with the situation. You may even alienate yourself from them and get even less cooperation in the future.

Instead, develop the habit of replacing complaining with asking for help and cooperation to ensure that the situation does not repeat itself. If the situation cannot be resolved, then go to a higher level, and if you are already making your point to the highest level of authority who cannot or will not help, then you may have to make the decision to sell your services to another organisation. Either way, things will then change. You have to create the situation and circumstances that will enable you to achieve your goals, not stand by and allow everything to happen to you.

Now it is time to get on to the practical techniques you want to learn to enable you to double your sales in six weeks.

ACTION POINTS

Get happy now—carry out the exercise in this chapter.

Make a commitment to stop making excuses and blaming other people. Take total responsibility for your life.

You can move straight on to the next chapter if you wish or just concentrate on getting into the habit of carrying out what you have learned to do so far for the next few days.

From this point on, please study and work on applying the techniques you will be taught one week at a time.

Chapter Three

Week One

Time Management

"Do not squander time for that is the stuff life is made of."
Benjamin Franklin

Time management is obviously not specifically a sales technique. However, if you could get fifty-percent more selling time out of your working week, the chances are that you could double your sales with just good time management skills.

There are numerous books you can read on this subject and, whilst they all contain some excellent advice, some can tend to get rather complex. In fact, one person who recently came to a workshop of mine complained to me that after attending a time management course, he was so busy managing his time that he had far less time available than he had before he attended the course. Therefore, in this chapter I am going to share with you the three simple techniques which I use to manage my time and which are the most effective that I know of.

Time Management Techniques

1 – Do Not Waste Your Time

There are three ways you can use your time. You can waste it, spend it or invest it. The only sensible way is the latter. One of the exercises I use at my conferences and workshops is to ask the audience to sit silently and watch the second hand of their wrist watch for exactly one minute. Then I explain that one minute of their life has just passed—and it is only if they learned the lesson not to waste time in the future that the minute was an investment. It is a simple and hard-hitting message.

One of the other questions I ask my audiences is: "As a percentage of your working day, how much time do you honestly admit to wasting or allowing other people to waste for you?" I ask them to write the answer down on a small piece of paper, fold it up so that their colleagues cannot see it, and then pass it down the row to the end where I have helpers collect them all. They are then put in a large box and I take twenty out of the box at random and read out the figures. I'd like you to write your figure down now before reading on.

The average time that those twenty people whose pieces of paper I pull out of the box admit to wasting or allowing other people to waste for them is a staggering twenty-four percent of their working day. What was your figure?

If you really want to double your sales, then one of the first and simplest things you can do is stop wasting time and, as a result, create more selling time.

Here is another exercise for you. Take two large sheets of paper and divide each into two columns. On the first sheet on the top of the right hand column write WAYS I WASTE MY TIME, and on the top of the other column write HOW I WILL DEAL WITH THIS IN FUTURE.

On the second sheet and at the top of the right hand column write WAYS I ALLOW OTHER PEOPLE TO WASTE MY TIME, and on the top of the other column write HOW I WILL DEAL WITH THIS IN FUTURE.

Ways you waste time could include:

Not having your current day fully planned the day before so you spend time planning it.

The solution could be: I will commit to planning every following day before I leave the office.

Reading an irrelevant magazine.

The solution could be: I will commit to only reading relevant trade magazines in the office and only when I am taking a tea or coffee break.

Shuffling business cards to see who you could telephone and who you would most like to telephone, instead of calling them all.

The solution could be: Start calling them right away and call them all. If you are never going to call them, dispose of their card so you never shuffle it again.

Making unnecessary telephone calls to kill time.

The solution could be: Commit to never killing time ever again.

Carry on until you have listed every single way that you waste time and how you will not waste it in the future. Then move on to the second sheet.

How you allow others to waste your time could include:

They come over to your desk with a cup of coffee in their hand and want to chat to you while they are drinking it and you are working.

The solution could be: Tell them politely that you have goals you want to achieve today and cannot spare the time.

They come and ask you for advice and say something like, "What would you do in this situation?"

The solution could be that you reply: "Why don't you go and think this through first, come back to me with your solution and I'll see if I agree."

Somebody invites you out for a spot of lunch.

I'm not saying lunch is for wimps but if you are going to have lunch, either have it with a customer or client, whilst networking, or alone and reading a useful book at the same time.

51

Carry on until you have listed every single way that you allow others to waste your time and how you will not allow them to waste it in the future.

When I carry this exercise out with people in a workshop the average time they decide they waste shoots up from the twenty-four percent before they had carried out this exercise to an even more staggering fifty-five percent! How did you do? How much extra time are you going to have available to you now? How much more are you going to be selling?

2 — The Fear Factor

I have already discussed fear with you, and now I want to relate it just to time management. I spend a lot of time in workshops questioning people as to why they waste time. I hear a lot of excuses but the one major reason why people waste time is rarely admitted until I finally mention it. That reason is FEAR!

Fear freezes people and stops them taking the action they should be taking. The moment you start feeling fear it connects with all the other fearful situations you have stored in your subconscious mind, and the more fear that comes up, the more non-positive you feel about everything that is going on around you. Maybe you can relate to the following story I was told by a workshop attendee when we discussed fear.

Susan told me that she had taken a large order from a new customer and really wanted to make a good impression. To that end, she took the order straight back to the office and ran a check to make sure that she could fulfil all the order requirements in the time frame promised to the customer. At eleven thirty in the morning she realised she had made a terrible mistake. Two of the fifteen items ordered were out of stock and could not be delivered on time and she had quoted a lower price than she should have on another.

She described herself as being in a state of shock and terrified of calling the customer and admitting the errors. She froze. She knew that the sooner she called was probably best, but she could not face making that call right away. The more she thought about it, the worse the implications became—a little like the story I told you earlier about Farmer Jones. She had non-positive words and imaginary conversations running through her mind. She pictured herself sitting at her office desk in a flood of tears with her boss reprimanding her, and the longer she thought about it, the worse she felt. She did not make the call that day and did very little other work either.

That evening she ate a hurried meal, went to bed early, slept badly and had awful dreams relating to her sales situation. The following morning when she arrived in the office she finally plucked up the courage to make the call. She apologised and explained that, in her eagerness to serve her customer well and promptly, she had made some statements immediately when she should have checked first with her office and then asked the customer what he would like to do next. He simply replied that she had made a really good impression on him, that he could wait the extra two weeks for delivery of the two items which were out of stock, and that the price difference on the other item would be OK. He also thanked her for being so apologetic, said he was concerned she seemed so upset and assured her they would be doing lots of business together in the future.

The moral to the story is simply that things are rarely ever as bad as you think they are going to be, and the more you think about them the less bad they are going to be in comparison to what you thought. So here is my second most effective time management technique—DO THE THINGS YOU FEAR MOST FIRST. When you do this and get the fearful things out of the way, the rest of the day becomes an absolute joy.

Do you dislike or fear cold calling but have to do it? Do you currently put it off until late in the day and sometimes leave the calls until the following day? All the time you delay, the fact you have to do it is still lurking in your subconscious mind and playing havoc with what should be a positive state.

Do you have some customers that you do not get on with too well and tend to give you a hard time when you call them? When will you call them now?

53

Do you get complaints from time to time? When will you deal with them now?

Here is what you should do when you carry out your planning for the following day's activities. List everything that you have to do, and then prioritise them in order of their fear factor. Those you fear most go to the top of the list and are carried out in that order. If, during that day, something else arises that has to be dealt with and is fearful, do it right away.

3 – The ISWAT Technique

You have one overriding primary goal right now, which is to double your sales in a time frame specified by you. So here is my final time management technique.

You need another pad of about twenty-five adhesive notes, but choose an alternative colour to yellow for this technique. Then write on them as I have illustrated below.

Place these alongside your yellow PDP adhesive notes where you will come across them frequently during the course of the day. Every time you are about to start on a new task or project, READ THE ISWAT NOTE! Ask yourself the question, 'Is what I am doing now or about to do going to help me achieve my goal?

ISWAT I am doing now or about to do going to help me achieve my goals?

If the answer is 'yes', you have three choices. You can do it right away, or you can allocate some specific time to do it later, or you may be fortunate enough to be able to delegate it to someone else, if that is appropriate.

If the answer is 'No—it is not going to help me achieve my goals', you have only one choice—dump it and dump it right away.

If it is another cup of coffee you are going to make—do not make it! If you are going to go and have a chat with a colleague about something unrelated to your goals—do not! If you are about to make a telephone call unrelated to achieving your goals—do not make the call! Focus only on what is going to help you to double your sales. If it is a telephone call from somebody you know who just wants to have a chat—politely hang up.

If you are looking at an e-mail that contains information you think you might look at later in case it just might be of some use in the future—delete it. If it is a piece of paper with some information on it which you think might be of use some time in the future, do not put it in the pile on your desk with other papers. Put it in the waste bin or shred it! If it is a magazine article you were about to read that is unrelated to your goal but the headline grabbed your attention—that goes in the bin too!

You have possibly heard the expression 'Clutter on the desk is clutter in the mind'. Once your conscious mind has seen an item of information, the fact that it exists is stored in your subconscious mind amongst the huge pile of other 'might do' information that is already stored there. It interferes with your focus. Clearing your desk and filing or hiding all this information in a filing cabinet or drawer does not help either. The subconscious mind still knows of its' existence. It has to be destroyed instantly! Of course you may occasionally destroy something that could have been of some use but that is nowhere near as bad as storing everything, just in case you might want to refer to it.

How many e-mails and other forms of correspondence do you receive every day? How quickly do people expect a response from you? Are you expected to justify every decision or recommendation you ever make with a mass of data to back them up?

I feel very strongly that we live in an age of information overload, unnecessarily rapid response requests and an irrational need to justify decisions or recommendations because so much information could be available to support these if we could find the time to research it.

The main cause of information overload is probably the internet. It is so easy to send an e-mail with attachments and at virtually no cost. So we are deluged with information that somebody thinks may be relevant to us but does not really care if it is or not because the time and cost of sending it is negligible. If we still worked in an age when people had to type and send letters written in correct English, with brochures and other accompanying information, I believe the flow of information we receive would be cut by approximately ninety percent and we would only receive information absolutely relevant to us. I also believe that we are expected to reply to e-mails and telephone calls far too rapidly. It is as if the person who is expecting the response has no respect for our time whatsoever. What is this doing to us as motivated and successful people with goals to achieve? Well, according to a recent survey, eighty percent of salespeople worked weekends, seventy-four percent worked whilst on annual leave and thirty-six percent had daily contact with their offices either by telephone or e-mail. Fifty-eight percent never took any exercise. How do you deal with this? Very simply and effectively, by using the ISWAT technique.

I also believe that we have come to expect to justify our decisions with data, even to ourselves. We have lost the art of using our most powerful and effective decision making tool, which is our 'Gut Feeling'. Take a leaf out of Richard Branson's book and his philosophy on business. Richard is one of the wealthiest and most successful business people on the planet and he was recently quoted as saying: "I never call in the accountants before making a decision. I make my decisions based on my gut feelings and then call in the accountants to make it work". Using the ISWAT technique is going to give you back your belief and trust in your gut feelings too.

The combination of these three techniques, applied diligently day by day, will create so much additional time for you. Combined with the other techniques you will learn week by week, you will easily double your sales!

ACTION POINTS

Stop wasting time—do the exercises detailed under this heading

Do the things you fear most first. Create your daily action plan on this basis

Implement the ISWAT technique

Continue with your PDP exercises daily

Do NOT move on to learning and applying anything in the next chapter. Just put into practice what you have learned this week.

Chapter Four

Week Two

Prospecting For New Customers

"New customers are the lifeblood of all successful businesses"
Dale Carnegie

This week we are going to deal with prospecting for new business. Depending upon what business we are in, we may call the people we sell to clients, customers or patients. For the sake of simplicity I will refer to them all as customers from this point onwards.

We are not going to cover advertising or marketing which are more passive activities and where you are either not involved or where there is likely to be little or no direct contact with the customer. Instead, we are going to be covering only those aspects of prospecting for new customers where you are directly involved and have total responsibility and control.

Cold Calling

If I ask an audience of one thousand people how many like and enjoy cold calling, no more than twenty hands will ever be raised. If that is the automatic response that is coming up from so many people's subconscious minds, it is any wonder that cold calling is ineffective for most people.

Now I accept that there are some companies who, mainly due to cost restraints, can only ever sell their products and services over the telephone. If you work in one of those organisations, then everything in this book can help you to achieve greater results. For the rest of us, who mainly cold call in order to introduce ourselves and to make appointments to see a prospective customer, I am going to make what might, at first, seem like a sweeping statement —COLD CALLING IS OVER.

Here are some of my reasons for this statement:

1. People who are paid to cold call for a living, and just to make appointments for other people, are usually paid in the region of about seven pounds an hour. That is the value the companies employing those staff put on their services. My first question to you is therefore "Do you rate your time as being worth more than that?" If you do, you should either be paying someone else to make the calls or ceasing cold calling altogether.

2. The people you are cold calling are likely to have a personal assistant or secretary you are going to have to speak with first or you are going to be put through to a voicemail. How much of your time do you want to spend speaking to secretaries or personal assistants with no authority to make a decision? How many times have you left messages on a voicemail asking for someone to return your call? How often have they called you back? I guarantee it's rarely been a good way to invest your time.

3. If you are cold calling a prospect you are initiating the call. The moment you do that, and assuming you get through, the prospect becomes defensive and sales resistance takes over. From that point on, the prospect and their subconscious mind are almost always going to go into sales resistance mode whenever you speak with them again and at every stage of the sales process.

4. Prospects fall into two categories. There are those who are scared of salespeople because they know they can be easily sold to. This category of prospects will rarely, if ever, take a cold call and, if they do, will be extremely defensive and unlikely ever to make an appointment. The other category are those who have no fear of salespeople, are happy to take calls from them to see how the salesperson promotes themselves and what they can learn from them and have no problems saying 'no'. If you do get an

appointment, the chances are that they will be with someone who is going to be very difficult to sell to indeed.

5. The last reason I am going to give you as to why cold calling is over, and there are many more, is very nicely summed up by the world famous entrepreneur Donald Trump, who said: "In selling you must never appear desperate, as soon as you look desperate, it's over".

Some of the hallmarks of professional and successful salespeople are that they come across as confident, assured, enthusiastic, in control and last and certainly not least—powerful. The mere fact that you have initiated the call, even though you do not like cold calling, implies that you do not have sufficient people you know to sell to already and consequently you send out the message —'I'm desperate'. As a result, you give up your confidence and assuredness, you sound less enthusiastic, you do not have control over the call and you do not have your power. What is the remedy? Never make a cold call ever again in an attempt to secure a potential customer. There are better ways.

Referral Prospecting

Fact: Word of mouth recommendations are the only form of advertising that most of us respond to any more.

To illustrate my point, when you last visited a restaurant you had not been to before, did you go because you saw an advertisement for it or because somebody recommended it to you? The last time you went to see a film was it because you saw an advertisement for it or because somebody told you it was great film and you really should see it? How about the last time you went to a shop to buy something? Was it because you saw an advertisement for the shop or because somebody told you it was great place to shop? Of course you may, from time to time, be persuaded by an advertisement or other form of advertising or marketing, but you are most likely to respond because somebody you know and whose judgement you trust, recommended you.

I also know that most people in sales ask for referrals, but in my experience it is a very 'hit and miss affair'. Asking for referrals is very rarely built into a salesperson's agenda for a conversation or meeting and is so often forgotten in the excitement of making a sale or the disappointment of losing one. From now on I want you to think of referrals in a completely different way. I want you to think of referrals as being more important than making a sale and I want you to make asking for them a formal part of your sales presentation.

This was a lesson I learned many years ago and very early in my sales career. I had just started working in the financial services sector and during my initial training my sales manager had constantly stressed the importance of obtaining referrals and shown me numerous techniques to obtain these.

I had been struggling for several weeks to make my first sale and when I had finally achieved that milestone, I hurried back to the office to present the completed application form to my sales manager. I remember the scene vividly to this day. I knocked on his door and asked if I might speak to him for a moment. He beckoned me in and I proudly placed the application form on his desk. "My first sale Bernie", I said. He removed his glasses, glanced down at the application form, looked up at me and said, "Well done Bruce; and how many referrals did you get?" Of course, in the excitement of getting my first sale, I had completely forgotten to ask for referrals. Then Bernie taught me a lesson I would never forget. "Bruce", he said, "this application will stay on my desk and will not be processed until you have gone back to the client and obtained at least three referrals." That is precisely what I had to do, what I did, and what a lesson I learned.

Some years later I developed a referral script for another large insurance company which salespeople are still taught some twenty years on. It was based on the concept of including an agreement to get referrals as part of the introduction. It went like this:

"I really appreciate the opportunity to meet with you (name) and see how I can be of assistance. May I first of all please just explain the way I work. What I'm going to do is carry out a detailed analysis of your current financial situation and, together with you, define precisely what your financial goals are. I am then going to go away, spend some time putting together a plan which will help you achieve those goals, and then have another meeting with you to explain my proposals. There is no charge for that work and I therefore do expect two things in return. One—that if you like my proposals you will go ahead and place the business with me and, two—that you will introduce me to three other people in similar circumstances to yourself, with a strong recommendation from you to them that they meet with me. Are you OK to go ahead on that basis?"

Not one person ever refused to go along with my terms and in most cases kept to the agreement. That approach of making it a condition of doing business with me was quite revolutionary in those days and still works extremely well today. Now we can do even better.

How To Ask For Referrals — Your Referral Script

The words you use when asking for referrals are critical, so learn these well.

When asking for referrals from someone who has not been referred to you:

> *"(John), I like to spend my time looking after my customers, not looking for them, so I would really appreciate your help please. Who else do you know who might also (be keen to double their sales—insert your key benefit here) that I should be speaking to please?"*

Now look carefully at the structure of this paragraph:

> *'(John)',* — *people like to hear the sound of their own name.*

> *'I like to spend my time looking after my customers, not looking for them'* — a reason and a benefit for them.

> *'so I would really appreciate your help'* — people like to help other people.

'Please' — one of the two most powerful words in the English language. The other is *'thank you'*.

When the person you are requesting referrals from is a referral themselves, adapted as follows it become even more effective:

> *"(John), I like to spend my time looking after my customers, not looking for them, so I would really value your help please. (Peter) introduced me to you and several other people and I would really appreciate it if you could do the same please. Who else do you know who might also (be keen to double their sales) that I should be speaking to please?"*

And if you really want to pack some more punch into it:

> *"(John), I like to spend my time looking after my customers, not looking for them, so I would really value your help please. (Peter) introduced me to you and seven other people and I would really appreciate it if you could do the same please. Who else do you know who might also (be keen to double their sales) that I should be speaking to please?"*

You may think this is a little cheeky but if you say it politely and warmly, you will be surprised at how effective this is. Just a few days ago I asked somebody this very question. His response was: *"I'm really sorry Bruce but I don't believe I could think of seven. But I could certainly come up with at least four or five."* *"Thank you very much"*, I said.

If you really want to double your sales, learn these off by heart so you never need to think about how you are going to ask for referrals again. I want to be able to wake you up at two-o-clock in the morning from a deep sleep and hear you say those words instantly.

The other psychological technique you should also use when asking for referrals is to have your pen out, poised over a piece of paper, ready to take notes of those referrals and in full view of your customer. When you do this, their conscious mind sees the picture of your pen poised over the paper and connects to something in their subconscious mind associated with that picture, which of course is to supply you with the information you have requested so that you can write it down. You are twice as likely to receive those referrals when you have the pen poised over the paper.

You should also do this when you are requesting referrals over the telephone. The fact that you have the pen poised over the paper connects with associations in your subconscious mind and affects the tone and pitch of your voice and how you speak when you make the request. How you speak also conveys to the other person's subconscious mind that you are holding a pen poised over a piece of paper. Hey presto—referrals as if by magic!

Now, one last thing on this subject of 'how to ask'. When you have got the names and contact details, explain that you do not like to call anyone unannounced and ask them to telephone the referral and make the introduction before you call, or e-mail them and copy you in. Ask them politely to do it that day. I promise you they will not be in the least bit offended and will comply with your request more often than not. Sometimes, if I think I can squeeze just a little more time out of the meeting, I will even ask them to make the calls while I am there.

When To Ask For Referrals

When I question an audience of salespeople about when they ask for referrals, approximately seventy percent raise their hands when I ask if they wait until the customer has placed an order with them. Ten percent confirm they sometimes ask during the sales process if it involves a series of meetings and things are going well. The remaining twenty percent either do not ask for referrals at all or will not raise their hands, no matter what I ask them.

Not once has anybody who has not heard me speak before ever thought of asking for referrals when they make contact with a potential customer for the first time. Well, now is the time for you to start doing just that. Picture the situation. You have made a cold call to a prospect (I'll forgive you this time) and you have got on reasonably well and you have made an appointment to go and see them. You have confirmed the date and time and that they have that in their diary. Here is what you must now say:

"(John), just one last thing. I like to spend my time looking after my customers, not looking for them, so just before I hang up, I would really appreciate your help please. Who else do you know in your area who might also (your key benefit here) that I should be speaking to please? I'd love to make contact with them and arrange to pop in for fifteen minutes to introduce myself while I'm there. Who can you think of please?" And don't forget your pen poised over a piece of paper.

If the person you are speaking to is a referral, then of course you adapt what you say as follows:

"(John), just one last thing. I like to spend my time looking after my customers, not looking for them, so just before I hang up, I would really appreciate your help please. Peter introduced me to you and several other people and I'd really appreciate it if you could do the same please. Who else do you know in your area who might also (your key benefit here) that I should be speaking to please? I'd love to make contact with them and arrange to pop in for fifteen minutes to introduce myself while I'm there. Who can you think of please?" And don't forget your pen poised over a piece of paper.

Some people will give you referrals, some will not. So what? You are no worse off than if you had not asked and I absolutely guarantee you that nobody will ever cancel an appointment they have just made because you asked for referrals before you had even met them. The fact is that they will admire and respect you for taking such a professional approach to the management of your time and will be looking forward to seeing you even more.

Supposing the person you are speaking to does not want to see you and will not make an appointment. Now what do you do. The answer is still ASK FOR REFERRALS. You have them in a weak moment. Nobody really likes to upset other people and, by turning you down, there's a good chance they are going to be even more likely to want to help you. So you say:

"(John), I really appreciate your honesty and not making an appointment with me that would have been a waste of both our time. Just one last thing—I like to spend my time looking after my customers, not looking for them and I would really value your help please. Peter introduced me to you and several other people and I'd really appreciate it if you could do the same please. Who else do you know in your area who might (your key benefit here) that I should be speaking to please?" And don't forget your pen poised over a piece of paper.

Once you get into the habit of asking for referrals before you meet and at every meeting, and when you have been turned down, and when you fail to make a sale at a presentation, you will quickly find you are making much more effective use of your time and sales will be increasing substantially. Just to get the point across to you one more time and even more powerfully, I can tell you that your future income will rise in direct proportion to the number of times you ask the referral question.

How To Encourage Even More Referrals

Now you have your customers giving you more referrals than you have ever had before, how are you going to encourage them to keep giving them to you so you have so much new business coming in that you do not ever have to think of making a cold call again? The answer is to look after that customer, and that means going the extra mile.

The first and most obvious thing you can do is to look out for potential customers for them. When you are with your customers and other prospective customers and when you are networking, always be thinking 'which of my customers could be selling to this prospect too?' Whenever you think there is a fit, here is what to say. Remember to look carefully at the way the following paragraph is constructed. It is full of positive statements and potential benefits to your prospect or customer.

"Mary, one of the things I also like to do is to help my customers to get more business whenever I can, and I'd like

to think I can do the same for you from time to time. Now one of my other customers, (Frank Jessup of ABC Supplies, offers the most fantastic service and prices on stationery), would you be OK to take a call from him and just explore if there's something you could be doing for each other?"

The other thing you can do is to keep your customers updated with new and important information relating to their business sector. You could be picking up this information from your Mastermind Group, from the daily newspapers, trade magazines and other sources. I find that by subscribing to Google News Alerts on subjects of interest to my customers, I can get the most up to date information delivered to my Inbox whenever I wish.

Now I am not suggesting you deluge your customers with information on a daily or weekly basis. Neither should you e-mail it to them because it will not appear to have great value to them in that format. What you should do, once every three or four weeks, is to print off what you consider to be the three very best articles you have come across. Put these in a neat plastic folder or one of your company's branded folders, hand write a note saying that you thought they might find this information useful, and put the package inside an envelope, hand write the address and post it to them or drop by and deliver it by hand. That way it really looks like you have gone to a lot of trouble. The more effort you can put into helping your customers to build their businesses, the more effort they are going to put in to helping you build yours.

To help summarise what we have covered on the subject of referrals so far, these are my Five Referral Rules:

1: Make giving you referrals a condition of your customers doing business with you.

2: Ask for referrals before you have met the potential customer.

3: Ask for referrals during the meeting with a potential customer.

4: Ask for referrals after meeting with the customer.

5: Encourage ongoing referrals from the customer.

WHAT ABOUT 'SUPPLIERS'?

Suppliers can be an equally good source of referrals and suppliers have a vested interest in keeping you happy. Let's face it—you are spending money with them!

When I first mention this subject in workshops there are some people who seem to have a resistance to it. But these are inevitably the people who have a resistance to asking for referrals in the first place. The other point that is often raised is that their suppliers deal in the business to consumer market whilst they deal in the business to businesses market—or vice versa. But all suppliers have many contacts in both those markets.

Last week I received a telephone call from a salesperson who had attended a workshop I ran several weeks before. Following my advice and during the following week, she had asked every supplier she spent money with for referrals. She asked the owner of her local corner store where she bought her morning newspaper. She asked the manager of her local supermarket where she did her weekly shop. She asked the person on the till at her local garage when she filled up with petrol. She asked the manager in the local DIY shop when she went in to purchase some screws she needed to put up a shelf. She asked her hairdresser when she went to have her hair styled and she asked the local dry cleaner when she went to pick up her clothes. In fact she asked every single person she came into contact with when she was buying from them.

Her approach was very straightforward. She would say "I'd really appreciate your help please. I don't know if I have told you this before but I sell security systems for offices and factories. Who do you know within about a fifty mile radius from here who runs a business that works from those type of premises?"

She also asked her manager for a list of suppliers the company used and has started to contact them. Within three weeks she told me that she had received over seventy-five new referrals and had stopped asking for the moment because she was simply too busy to follow them all up.

So here are some Five Additional Referral Rules for you:

1: Make giving you referrals a condition of your suppliers doing business with you. If they won't - change suppliers.
2: Wherever possible, ask for referrals before you have met the potential supplier.
3: Ask for referrals during the meeting with a supplier.
4: Ask for referrals after meeting with a supplier.
5: Encourage ongoing referrals from a supplier.

NETWORKING

The only other prospecting technique I want to share with you is networking, something that I am sure you are familiar with because networking has become a rapid growth industry in its' own right. We have online networking organisations such as Ecademy and Facebook, which have tens, if not hundreds of thousands of members. We have offline organisations running face to face meetings such as BNI, BRX, The Academy of Chief Executives, and many others, some of which have become worldwide franchise organisations generating millions in income for the franchisees. It's quite obvious that networking works. I would therefore like to share some ideas to hopefully make it work a lot better for you.

Your Introduction

Whether you are attending a formal networking meeting, or you just happen to be out for a drink after work with a friend who introduces you to someone they know, or you are at a party or any other event, at some time somebody is going to ask you 'what do you do?' I hear this question asked of so many people, so many times, and I know it has been asked of them many times before. I am flabbergasted that most people still struggle to answer the question and are very rarely able to give a brief and exciting description of what they do in a way which makes people want to know more. So that is our first task.

I want you to a write a brief description of what you and the business you represent can do for other people, one which you can be proud of, which excites other people and can be expressed in less than fifteen seconds. This is known as an 'elevator pitch'. Then I want you to write another that would take you a little longer, can be more descriptive and finally a third which can take a little longer still. That last one is the 'tall building elevator pitch'.

Your introductions need to be powerful and based on the WIIFM factor (What's In It For Me — the potential customer). It does not necessarily matter what your company's name is unless it's a brand that everyone wants to deal with - it is your name that counts. It does not matter if your business was established in 1944. That does not mean you do a great job because you have been around a long time. The only thing that matters is that you have something to say which mentions a problem you can solve and might inspire the potential customer you are talking to, or someone they know, to find out more about what you can do for them. Here are three examples of my own elevator pitches which illustrate the way they can be constructed.

> "I'm Bruce King. I help salespeople who are struggling to meet or exceed their targets to increase their sales by at least fifty percent in three weeks."

> "I'm Bruce King. I help salespeople who are struggling to meet or exceed their targets. I inspire and motivate them and give them techniques to enable them to increase their sales by at least fifty percent in three weeks."

> "I'm Bruce King. I help salespeople who are struggling to meet or exceed their targets. I work with anything from small groups to large audiences of two thousand or more. I inspire and motivate them and give them techniques to enable them to increase their sales by at least fifty percent in three weeks."

Do you think these might create some interest if the person I was saying them to was either in sales themselves, employed a sales team or organised conferences? I can assure you it does.

Let me give you a few more illustrations of how this should be done, using some 'before' and 'after' examples to show you how

I adapted other people's descriptions to take them from boring to exciting. These are just the brief versions:

BEFORE: I'm Susan Scott from Susan Scott Training. I do team building.

AFTER: I'm Susan Scott. I help fragmented teams align around a common vision to create greater profitability.

BEFORE: I'm a mortgage broker with First National Finance.

AFTER: I'm Kevin Walters. I help first time buyers who are struggling to get financing for the home of their dreams.

BEFORE: I'm Mary McDonnell. I'm with XYZ Medical Equipment. We were established in 1944 and we sell cardiac resuscitation equipment.

AFTER: I'm Mary McDonnell. I sell equipment to medics and paramedics that helps to save thousands of lives a year.

BEFORE: I'm John Spiers with Ellingberg CRM Systems. I sell and implement fully integrated CRM systems that are compatible with all major database applications and which are utilised by FT100 companies.

AFTER: I'm John Spiers. I help large organisations manage their customer information to reduce customer turnover and drive repeat sales.

Now create your own introductions for your products or services and when you are really pleased with them, learn them off by heart. I should be able to wake you at two-o-clock in the morning from a deep sleep and you should be able to repeat your introductions instantly and with enthusiasm. Then whenever anyone asks you, 'what do you do?', you will have that exciting and stimulating answer without having to think about it and lose the moment. You just never know whom you are speaking with and whether what you do may be of interest to them, or someone they know.

BECOME A POWER NETWORKER

I often come across people who have attended numerous formal business networking events and have decided that 'networking doesn't work'. The truth of the matter is that networking does work and that it is they who have failed to make it work for them.

If you have ever been to a formal networking event, then the following scenario may be familiar to you.

A business person, let's call him John, arrives at the networking event venue. There is a large sign over the door which says 'Networking Event' — a final reminder of what John is there for before he enters. Once inside, John looks nervously around at the forty or fifty people mingling and chatting to each other and finally sees somebody he knows from a previous networking event and heads over to talk to them. After ten to fifteen minutes of idle chatter John decides he has to get on with some real networking and parts company. John then looks around again and sees someone standing alone and obviously feeling uncomfortable, so he goes over to introduce himself. It becomes obvious after just a minute or so that this person is rather boring, has little genuine interest in what John does and probably knows very few people, if any, who would be interested in what John has to offer. Nevertheless, because John does not want to appear rude and is himself a little nervous with networking, he stays and chats to this gentleman for another fifteen minutes before excusing himself. John repeats this 'networking dance' four or five more times during the evening before deciding the event is a waste of time, and leaves with five or six business cards which will almost certainly lay untouched in a drawer for several months before being discarded.

If that scenario was familiar to you because that is how you often conduct yourself at networking events, then stop it! Of course it does not work. I am going to share with you how to network successfully so that you create a network of people who do business with you and, more importantly, constantly refer you to many other people who will do business with you. Before I do that, let us take a look at some networking basics.

73

First of all, there are two reasons for attending a networking session; the first is to meet people who may want to transact business with you and the second is to meet people who may be able to introduce you to other people who want to do business with you.

Secondly, other successful and well connected people you meet at a networking session are unlikely to remember very much about you the following day, no matter how much of an impact you make at the time.

Thirdly, even if they do remember you, they are unlikely to remember enough about you to telephone you and ask you to discuss doing business with you and they definitely do not know enough about you to recommend you to other people. It takes most people at least an hour of face to face conversation with you before they might start referring you to their contacts, and the more they value their reputation, the longer it may take. You have to prove to them you are referable!

On the basis of those points, you may well ask, 'what is the point of networking then?' It took me about two years to develop a contact list of over five thousand people I met at networking events before I realised that I was doing something wrong. I finally learned that the purpose of attending a networking event was to meet as many people as possible and to select just a few from the many I met whom I believed were active networkers themselves, were successful or working hard at becoming successful, that I liked when I first met them and were people I wanted to spend some time getting to know a lot better and helping them to get to know me a lot better. When you start looking at people and talking to people with that in mind, it soon becomes very easy to identify them at networking events.

Now let us take a look at how John should be working a networking event. This time John strides into the room looking positive and at ease. He notices a few people standing alone sipping glasses of wine, looking a little dejected, avoiding eye contact and ignores them. He then sees a couple of smartly dressed business people talking animatedly and enthusiastically and heads straight towards them. On the way he notices two other people he has met before, one who he has not followed up and another who has become a client. He stops briefly to say a very polite and friendly hello but it is obvious from his manner that he is about to move on quickly, which he does. He approaches the two strangers and stands just a little distance from them, but close enough that he is almost part of the conversation. They of course then notice him, take a brief pause in their conversation and turn to look at him. He then takes his opportunity to speak. *"Hello I'm John Stevens. I couldn't help noticing you both and as we haven't met before, I thought I'd just drop over and introduce myself. I do hope I'm not interrupting."*

Within the space of fifteen minutes, John has introduced himself, found out what businesses the other two people are involved with, explained what he does and exchanged business cards with them. He has also decided their rating from one to five; a rating of one being 'not worth following up' and a rating of five being 'definitely worth speaking to again'. He also finds it very easy to extricate himself from this little meeting because he interrupted it in the first place. So he simply says *"I'm going to leave you gentleman to carry on with what you were discussing before I interrupted you. It was a pleasure to meet you and, if you don't have any objections, I would love to chat with you in the next day or two and see what we might be able to do to help each other. Would that be OK?"* And of course it is.

During the next few hours, John joins several other couples and threesomes who are in conversation and by the end of the evening has introduced himself to over thirty people, exchanged business cards with them and has made a note on their cards of their one to five score.

The following day, John goes through those business cards, selects out the seven people he scored either a four or five and calls them with a view to meeting for an hour or so to really get to know each other. John has become a power networker.

FORM YOUR OWN MASTERMIND GROUP

We have already discussed that there are countless opportunities for networking and I encourage you to attend as many of these as you can and make them work for you as John does. I also encourage you to form your own Mastermind Group. Here is what you should do.

Your intention should be to form a group of ten to twelve people who commit to meet once every two weeks for a two-hour breakfast session. The purpose of these sessions will be three-fold.

1: To exchange market knowledge
2: To introduce potential customers to each other
3: To discuss any particular challenges anyone in the group may be having and advise accordingly.

The people you want in your group should be from companies who are likely to be serving customers in a similar sector to your own but are not in competition with each other. For example, if you sell office furniture, you would be looking to invite salespeople or sales directors who sell carpeting, stationery, computer systems, IT networking solutions, copying equipment, mailroom services, office electrical installations, telephone systems, mobile communication solutions, etc.

Put together a list of appropriate organisations in your district and then telephone their sales director. Explain that you are putting together this Mastermind Group, the purpose of it, and that you would like to invite them or one of their top salespeople to attend an introductory meeting. You want the best person, not the worst person or somebody who is struggling. If you want to double your sales you want to be flying with the eagles, not twittering with the sparrows!

The purpose of the introductory meeting is to get a commitment from everyone to the three principles and to attend regularly. Then you have your Mastermind Group.

ACTION POINTS

Stop cold calling

Create and learn your Referral Scripts

Ask for referrals before you have met a potential customer and every time you meet with them

Keep your eyes open for market information and potential customers for your customers — *practise*

Ask for referrals from all of your suppliers. If they cannot or will not help, change suppliers.

Create and learn your 15 second Introduction

Become a Power Networker

Form your own Mastermind Group

Continue with your PDP exercises daily

Do NOT move on to learning and applying anything in the next chapter. Just put into practice what you have learned this week and last week.

Chapter Five

Week Three

Improving Your Communication Skills

"The goal of effective communication should be for
someone to say, 'yes please' rather than 'so what?'"
Bruce King

At the beginning of this week, I am going to take you through
the different psychological profiles of the typical prospect and
how to tailor your sales presentation to them. There are two main
categories and several sub-categories. We will deal with the two
main categories first.

The Psychological Profile Of Buyers

The Conceptual Buyer And The Analytical Buyer

Picture the scene. You have an appointment with the managing
director of a privately owned manufacturing company whose
premises are situated on a modern, purpose-built factory estate
just outside town. The first thing you notice is the neat, clearly
marked parking spaces in the forecourt. You pull up in the space
marked 'visitors' and your eye is caught by the car parked in the
space marked J. Higgins. Mr Higgins is your prospect and drives a
one-year-old luxury saloon car that is very clean and obviously well
maintained.

The reception area is well laid out and tidy. There are several nicely
framed reproductions of modern art on the wall. The receptionist

is polite, makes you feel welcome, offers you a cup of coffee and announces your arrival to your prospect's secretary. Ten minutes later Mr Higgins' secretary comes down to collect you and takes you up for your first meeting with Joe Higgins.

As you enter his office you quickly take in the smart carpets and office furnishing. There are more pictures on the walls, one or two of which appear to be limited editions that have been signed by the artist. There are several golfing trophies on the bookcase and a photograph that appears to be Mr Higgins standing by a yacht and collecting a trophy.

Mr Higgins stands up to greet you with a friendly but cautious smile, extends his hand, offers a firm handshake and bids you sit down in a comfortable, upright, visitor's chair on the opposite side of the desk to himself. He is dressed smartly. He wears a fairly expensive suit, a well-ironed, pale blue shirt with a modern tie, and he is well groomed.

The desk itself is very neat and tidy, particularly for the owner of a medium-sized manufacturing company. There is a small pile of drawings on one side, held down by a very ornate, modern glass paperweight. Several other sketches are in front of him. A note-pad on the desk is covered with various, abstract doodles. In a corner of the office, behind the desk is a slightly untidy pile of files. In the opposite corner, a briefcase lies open. It is literally littered with odd scraps of paper, bills, taxi receipts and other paraphernalia.

Mr Higgins is a typical 'conceptual' buyer, not so much concerned with facts or figures. He makes almost instant decisions. If he wants something, and as long as he thinks he can afford it, he will buy it. He may not even haggle over the price. Provided you hit the right hot button, he will possibly have talked himself into the sale before you even attempt to close him.

Mr Higgins is concerned with overall appearances, hence the cordial welcome when you first arrive, the neat and fairly expensive furnishings in his office, his smart, somewhat trendy and well-groomed appearance and the various paintings, photographs and trophies which adorn the walls and bookcase.

The other significant clues to his 'conceptual' category are the doodles on the note-pad, the pile of files in the corner of the office and the very untidy briefcase, coupled with the fairly tidy desk and the noticeable absence of very much other paperwork.

Next, picture another scene, very different from this. Your appointment with Mr Jones is scheduled for ten minutes past eleven, at his request. At precisely ten past eleven, Mr Jones enters the reception area, mumbles for you to follow him to his office, promptly turns his back to you and leads the way.

Mr Jones is wearing a shabby suit that has obviously not been pressed for some time. His shoes are somewhat worn down at the heel and his hair looks as if it was last cut at about the same time that his suit was last pressed.

On entering his office you immediately notice its unkempt and untidy appearance. Everything is dowdy and looks as if it should have been replaced at least two or three years ago. There are no frills, no pictures on the wall, no magazines on the coffee-table and only technical books on the bookshelf. The desk is covered with piles of papers in an order that is obviously logical to Mr Jones but would make little sense to anyone else. Most of them are covered with figures and various calculations. The writing is neat and precise and all the additions appear to have been double-checked and annotated in red ink to indicate their accuracy.

Mr Jones is, of course, the complete opposite to Mr Higgins. Mr Jones is an 'analytical' buyer. Left to his own devices, and in the absence of any salespeople to bother him, he probably would not change the office carpet or furniture for another twenty years. By the time he had worked out his budgets and decided whether or not he could afford them, prices would no doubt have gone up and he would have thought of a dozen different reasons why he did not need a change.

Mr Jones does not spend money unnecessarily, at least in his business life. His personal habits, however, may be very different. His office is untidy and so is he. However, take a look at the columns of figures on the documents piled on his desk and you realize that

Mr Jones knows exactly what is happening in every part of his organisation and has his finger very much on the pulse. He does not make snap decisions or snap judgements. Try to close him on an idea without any data to back it up and you will get nowhere.

These are two extreme examples of the two main categories of prospects that you can come across. If you think Mr Higgins is a salesperson's dream, you could not be further from the truth. Press the wrong hot button and you could switch his interest off very quickly indeed. Try and impress him with too many facts, figures or statistics and you will bore him and possibly never regain his interest.

Mr Jones, on the other hand, will require a lot of technical information and other facts and figures to support your statements. Some variations of Mr Jones can actually be a lot easier to close than Mr Higgins, provided you know how to handle them.

So there we have it. Two main categories of buyer: the conceptual and the analytical. Just being able to identify these two types quickly when first meeting them can significantly increase your chances of making that sale. It will, however, take a little time and practice before you get it right every time and the distinction between the conceptual buyer and the analytical one is not always as obvious as in the examples above. There is often a little of Mr Jones in Mr Higgins and a little of Mr Higgins in Mr Jones.

The key, of course, is observation. You must be acutely aware of how your prospect behaves, his style of dress, the environment of his workplace where appropriate, and any other factors that can help you decide quickly whether the person you are about to sell to is a conceptual or analytical buyer.

THE PSYCHOLOGICAL SUB-CATEGORIES

To give you an even greater edge, we need to examine the various sub-categories of buyers which appear in either of the main categories. These are Grumpy, Friendly, Timid, Procrastinator, Snob and, finally, the Dealer.

The Grumpy Buyer

Grumpy buyers are obviously not very difficult to identify. They tend to be miserable and complain a lot, often about things that are totally irrelevant to your company and your sales presentation. They will almost always see the worst in any situation instead of the best, and are inclined to think that things will go wrong rather than right. They always have problems and are cautious, cost conscious and, of course, grumpy.

The secret to dealing with people in this category is to be sympathetic. You must show concern for their concerns, agree with them wherever possible and never argue. Arguing only makes them worse. However, almost every time you do agree and show sympathy or concern, reinforce what your product or service can do to solve their problems.

The Friendly Buyer

The Friendly buyer is almost everybody's friend. People in this sub-category like to be liked. They like to tell stories and to get involved in long conversations that often have nothing to do with business. They are always pleased to see most people who call on them and, because they are so friendly and easy to get along with, you may think that a sale is inevitable. Nothing could be further from the truth.

The friendly buyer is more likely to use the time allotted for your meeting to enjoy a long, friendly chat and then whisk you out of the door with a hearty pat on the back, a big smile and no order. They are so good at this that, no matter how many times you call, they will do the same thing time after time.

The secret of dealing with the friendly buyer is quite simple. You must, of course, be friendly, but your friendliness must be controlled. Once you have decided whether your buyer is the analytical or conceptual type, tailor your presentation accordingly and be friendly but firm. Do not allow yourself to be side-tracked into conversations that are not related to business. If you can double the amount of time you spend selling rather than listening to or swapping stories, you could double the size of the order.

The Timid Buyer

Timid buyers are not timid because of their physical size; they come in all shapes and sizes. They are timid because of the way they think. Their one outstanding characteristic is that they are scared. They are scared of making decisions, of change, of making mistakes, of the competition—and they are probably absolutely petrified of salespeople.

Nevertheless, timid buyers, once recognized, are also easy to deal with. The secret is never to scare them. This means that, above all else, you must take your time. As with the friendly buyer, you have to stay on track, but you must also slow down your sales presentation to a rate that is even slower than your prospect would like it to be. Doing so will prompt them to ask questions and get involved in the sales process. They will quickly begin to feel that they are in charge, possibly for the first time ever, and will become very easy to sell to.

Once you feel that they are ready to buy, you must not offer them a choice. Remember that, above all else, timid buyers are scared of making decisions and it is therefore up to you to make decisions for them. Do not ask for the sale because you are unlikely to get it. Assume that they are going to buy and just write up the order, push the order form across to them and tell them to authorize it.

The Procrastinating Buyer

People in this sub-category just cannot make up their minds about anything. It is not because they are scared. It is simply part of their psychological make-up. In their private and business lives procrastinators always ask other people's opinions and, very often, ask other people to make the decisions for them.

To sell to the procrastinator, you simply must make them a friend and gain their trust. Once they are comfortable with you, they will give you the opportunity to make the decision for them. At the slightest sign of a buying signal, tell them what they should be doing and close the sale.

The Snobbish Buyer

The snob is a totally different character. Snobs look down their noses at most people and often consider salespeople to be a lower life-form that is hardly deserving of their time or energy. They need very careful handling but they have two major traits for you to capitalize on. First, they think they know it all, and there is no fool like a 'know all'. Second, although they pretend to know everything, deep down they are often very insecure and have an avaricious need to learn.

The clever way to deal with snobs is to flatter them. By complimenting them on their knowledge of your product or service, and feeding back a little more information each time, you can easily lead them into a closing situation. However, you must remember that snobs never like to be sold to. You must therefore make sure that you phrase your closing question in such a way that the snob believes he or she has decided to buy.

Remember, too, that snobs like to be thanked. Thank them for seeing you, thank them for their interest, thank them for just about anything you can thank them for. Then thank them again for the order when you leave.

The Dealer Buyer

Our final category is the dealer. Dealers just love to deal. They want the very best price you can offer, the best service and the best delivery. When you have agreed to everything, and given away most of your profit, they will want even more and there will still be no guarantee that they are going to buy from you.

Do not confuse a dealer with a negotiator. Most people like to negotiate the best offer they can for themselves. In many cases, if they are working for a company, it is their responsibility to obtain the best they can for their employer. That is what they are paid to do. A dealer's psychology is very different and dealers are unique among the categories we have discussed. They can be the toughest negotiators, but their weak spots make them the easiest category to sell to.

85

First, dealers do not like to waste time unnecessarily. If they start to deal, even on very minor points during your initial approaches, they must be interested in what you have to offer. Second, they have an over-abundance of pride, and hate to go back on their word once they have given it. Third, they tend to be in a hurry. To secure a sale with a dealer, you need to arouse his or her interest, create a sense of urgency and get a commitment at every single stage of your presentation. You will then always be able to take a step back in your negotiation and remind them that they made that commitment. They will rarely go back on their word.

Once you have decided whether the dealer is a conceptual or analytical buyer, and provided you follow the simple sequence of arousing interest, creating urgency and getting frequent commitments, you will possibly have more fun dealing with the dealer than with any other type of prospect. In addition, because of their nature, dealers tend to hold some of the most powerful positions in trade and industry and have some of the largest purchasing budgets. Learn to deal with the dealer and you can easily become one of the highest paid people in sales.

This week, as well as having showed you how to identify the various prospect types and communicate and sell to them, I am going to teach you some other techniques that will work so very well for you and will enable you to make a lot of extra sales, no matter what prospect type you are dealing with.

THE COMMUNICATION MODEL

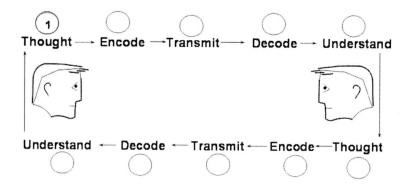

Look at the diagram on the previous page which illustrates how verbal communication takes place. Starting at point 1 (top left) the first person has a thought. They then encode that; in others words they put their thoughts into words. They then transmit their words (speak). The person who they are talking to hears the words and decodes them in a way they can understand, has their own thoughts which are then encoded, transmitted, and so the process goes on. If you consider that cycle, apart from the initial thought (1), the only part of the communication process you can be fairly sure people get right is the transmission. Even then some people do not actually say the words they had intended. So is it any wonder that communication is fraught with difficulty. It's a little like playing Chinese whispers.

Communication is further complicated by the fact that we are not understood solely by the words we use. According to behavioural psychologists, during face to face conversation, the words we use account for only ten percent of our communication. Thirty-five percent of communication is how we say those words, and the remaining fifty-five percent is how we look when we speak.

When we are communicating on the telephone, the percentages change to:

Words: twenty percent

How we speak: fifty-five percent

How we look: twenty-five percent.

Yes—even when people cannot see us they are creating visual images of how they think we look and what we are doing. Most of this goes on subconsciously but it is definitely happening. If we are distracted and maybe doodling on a pad, our voices change a little. The other person's subconscious mind picks up on these nuances and tells their conscious mind you are not paying proper attention to them. People can 'sense' when you are not behaving as you should be, which leads me to my first Communication Rule...

When speaking with someone on the telephone—act as if you were really there!

87

Do everything you would do as if you were sitting face to face with the customer and do not do anything you would not do if you were face to face with them. By acting in this manner you will enhance the positive effect of your communications significantly and dramatically increase the likelihood of achieving the desired outcome of your call.

Some time ago, I was asked to see what I could do to help a small, struggling telephone marketing company to increase their sales. The salary and commissions being paid to these salespeople were excellent but the offices where the sales team were based were untidy, dreary, not a very inspiring place to work, and the team were dressed terribly. In some cases they looked as if they had just got out of bed.

I explained my theories to the Managing Director and we had the offices redecorated and inspirational posters framed and placed around the room. Then we asked the salespeople for their co-operation. With their agreement, we introduced a timetable that allowed six ten-minute coffee breaks a day in addition to the lunch break, and banned drinking and eating at all other times. We gave them the title 'Telephone Sales Executives' and they agreed to dress for work in a businesslike fashion. The men would wear business suits, shirts and ties, the women, skirts or smart slacks and blouses. Anyone who did not have suitable clothes or the money to buy them was given an interest-free loan. At the end of the first week under this new regime sales were up forty-two percent.

How To Establish Immediate Rapport

According to behavioural psychologists, people make a decision on whether they like and trust people within less than ten seconds of first meeting them or speaking with them. One of the most important things you should want to do is to establish rapport with a prospect as quickly as you possibly can. The faster you can establish rapport, the more likely you are to close a sale.

From this point on in this book, it is important to understand that whenever I mention the words 'close a sale' that does not necessarily mean that you take an order that day. More often than not it is going to take two or more meetings with your prospect in order to 'close a sale'. So 'close a sale' could also mean getting an agreement to move on to the next stage of the sales process, as well as taking an order.

How can we establish an immediate rapport with a prospect? In this section I am going to share with you two Neuro-Linguistic Programming (NLP) techniques. Over the last twenty years, NLP has come to the fore as a most powerful communication and influencing skill. When I first developed the techniques I am going to share with you, I had not heard about NLP and just developed them myself on the basis of my own experiences of learning to communicate and influence people. When NLP became more well known, I studied it with great interest and there are many more NLP techniques available to you than I am going to describe here. However, having studied them all myself, I know that the two I am going to share with you are the two most effective and all you really need to know in order for you to double your sales.

NLP Technique 1 – Mirroring & Pacing

Before NLP there was a phrase often used in the sales profession that described the best salespeople as 'like chameleons' in that they became like their prospects—in other words they mirrored the other person in every way.

The effectiveness of mirroring is based on the simple fact that most people like to do business with people they like and trust, and the people they most like and trust are people who are most like themselves. They may admire people with different personality traits, mannerisms, ways of speaking and for the way they look, but they feel more comfortable doing business with people who are just like them. Thus, the objective when you use this technique is to make the person you are selling to think that they are looking in a mirror and seeing themselves. Mirroring enables you to get in direct contact with your prospect's subconscious mind, and have their subconscious mind say to them, 'This person is just like me. I like them, I trust them and I believe I can do business with them'.

In order to mirror someone effectively, there are four things that you can do. The first is to copy their physical actions and mannerisms. If you are greeted with a firm handshake, respond with a firm one. If the handshake is weak, yours must also be weak. If your prospect remains standing with a hand in their pocket, you remain standing with a hand in your pocket. If your prospect sits forward in their chair, you sit forward. If they sit with their arms folded—never mind what you have been told about body language in the past—you sit with your arms folded.

If your prospect crosses their legs, you cross yours. If he or she starts to fiddle with a pen, do the same. Everything you do during the course of your meeting with a prospective client that mimics what he or she is doing will help to cement a relationship with that person more quickly than anything you might say.

In case you are thinking what I think you are thinking—you will never be spotted. You can master this technique in just a few days and mirror what the other person is doing without it ever being noticed. In fact, the more like someone you are, the less likely they are to notice it. However, their subconscious mind will be noticing all the time. Their subconscious minds will be telling them that they like you, that they trust you and that they would like to do business with you. From that point on, selling to them just gets easier and easier.

Have you ever taken a call from someone who was trying to interest you in their company's product and service and, within the space of a few seconds, found there was something about them that really irritated you and you knew that no matter what they were offering, you did not want it? Well the bad news is that you have almost certainly had precisely the same effect on someone else. That is disturbing, is it not?

The reason this happens is that there is something about your voice or their voice, and possibly the words you or they have used, that deeply irritates the subconscious mind. So the next most powerful mirroring technique is to match your prospect's rate, tone and pitch of speech.

If your prospect speaks quickly, then you speak quickly too. If they speak slowly, you speak slowly. If they sound upbeat and excited, you mirror that and sound upbeat and excited. If they sound a little subdued then you sound subdued too. As soon as you have established rapport you can begin to sound a little more upbeat and they will become upbeat and more positive too. If they have a deep voice, lower the pitch of your voice to match it. If they have a higher pitched voice, raise the pitch of yours a little also. By mirroring your prospect's rate, tone and pitch of speech you are sending a message to their subconscious mind that you are just like them and it is OK for them to like you, trust you and do business with you.

The other two techniques you can use, which are not necessarily quite as important but can also have a dramatic impact on the effectiveness of your communication with your prospect, is to mirror what they wear and what they eat.

With regards to what they wear, I am not suggesting that you should be silly enough to start dressing as somebody of the opposite sex or copying precisely what you know they are likely to be wearing so you look like twins. However, I do want you to be conscious of not being overdressed or underdressed. For example, I recently taught this technique to a salesperson who was struggling to meet his targets selling animal feed to farmers, as indeed were most of his colleagues. He tried out my suggestion of swapping his designer raincoat and smart leather shoes for a green Barbour mackintosh and Wellington boots. His sales increased by thirty percent just by this change in his dress code. Neither did he have to spend hours scraping the mud off his shoes and polishing them every day.

Another, who sold into the record industry, had always dressed like a city gent. He was very smart and conventionally dressed and looked rather out of place in a meeting of trendy entertainment executives who never wore ties. Although he was slightly older than many of his prospects, getting him to dress a little more like them with a designer suit and very smart, but trendy, shirts without a tie, enabled him to increase his sales by twenty-three percent almost immediately.

What about mirroring what prospects eat? If you are offered tea or coffee, choose what your prospect chooses. If they put sugar in their tea or coffee, you do the same. It does not matter if you have to put three teaspoons of sugar in your tea when you do not usually take sugar. It is worth putting up with if it will help you close that sale. The fact that you are drinking the same beverage as your prospect, no matter how revolting you may find it, will help to reinforce in their subconscious mind that you are similar to them and that they like you, trust you and can do business with you.

I explained this technique to a book publisher one morning. She was very concerned about a lunch meeting she was having with a buyer from a major department store. In the past, he had always been very difficult to get on with and reluctant to place more than just a small order with her.

The publisher called me back later that day. She told me that she had tried, but found it very difficult to copy the buyer's mannerisms and the way they spoke. She had, however, not found it difficult to order the same food and drink as her prospect. Apparently, by the time the dessert trolley came around and she ordered the strawberries and cream, without sugar, as her prospect had, he was virtually eating out of her hand. She came away with the biggest order she had ever received from that buyer and, in addition, developed a completely different relationship with him that, over the next few years, made her a great deal of money.

By mirroring your prospect's style of dress and what they eat and drink, you are sending a message to their subconscious mind that you are just like them and it is OK for them to like you, trust you and do business with you.

NLP Technique 2 — Mirroring & Leading

You may be thinking to yourself, 'how will I know for certain when I have established rapport with someone?' Most times, you tend to get a gut feeling that you are establishing a good rapport with your prospect, but the way to be certain is to test it. If you have been mirroring your prospects body language and you believe you have established rapport, test it by pulling on your ear lobe, or tapping your pen or some other movement or action. If your prospect copies you within a few moments, you know that you have established absolute rapport. Once you know that, you can then increase your pace a little, start to speak a little faster and a little more excitedly and if your prospect follows your lead and mirrors you, you will find it much easier to excite them and want them to buy your product or service.

MATCHING COMMUNICATION MODES

Have you ever gone to a meeting where you had qualified the prospect thoroughly, you knew your product would be immensely useful to them and that they had the money and the authority to buy and you were convinced they would—and yet they did not and you could not fathom why they turned you down? You may be about to find out the reason why they said no.

People communicate and make decisions in one of three different ways. Some people experience, understand and make decisions based upon the words and sounds they 'hear'. When they are thinking things through they run the words through their conscious minds and talk to themselves. The technical term for this is an 'auditory' person.

Others experience, understand and make decisions based upon what they 'see'. When they are thinking things through they run the pictures through their conscious minds and create pictures. The technical term for this is a 'visual' person.

The third group experience, understand and make decisions based upon what and how they 'feel' about something. The technical term for this is a 'kinaesthetic' person.

We all use all three of these communication modes, but one is almost always far more dominant than the other two. To find out which is your dominant communication mode, complete the following questionnaire. There are fifteen sections and you need to select the one response that most appeals to you in each section. Do this as quickly as possible because the faster you respond to the questions, the more accurate the results will be. When you have completed all fifteen, total the number of A, B and C responses.

IN THE LIST BELOW, TICK THE RESPONSE THAT INSTANTLY MOST APPEALS TO YOU:

1.

A: I love to listen to music. ☐

B: I enjoy art galleries & window shopping. ☐

C: I feel compelled to dance to good music ☐

2.

A: I would rather take an oral test than a written test. ☐

B: I was good at spelling in school. ☐

C: I tend to answer questions using my gut feeling. ☐

3.

A: I've been told I have a good speaking voice. ☐

B: My confidence increases when I look good. ☐

C: I enjoy being touched. ☐

4.

A: I can resolve problems more quickly when I talk out loud. ☐

B: I would rather be shown an illustration than have something explained to me. ☐

C: I find myself holding or touching things as they are being explained. ☐

5.

A: I can usually tell someone's sincerity from the tone of their voice. ☐

B: I find myself evaluating people based on their appearance. ☐

C: The way others shake hands means a lot to me ☐

6.

A: I would rather listen to cassettes than read books. ☐

B: I like to watch TV and go to the movies. ☐

C: I like hiking and other outdoor activities. ☐

7.

A: I can hear the slightest noise that my car makes ☐

B: It's important that my car is clean inside and out. ☐

C: I like a car that feels good when I drive it. ☐

8.

A: Others tell me that I'm easy to talk to. ☐

B: I enjoy "People Watching". ☐

C: I often touch people when talking to them. ☐

9.

A: I am aware of what voices sound like on the telephone as well as face to face. ☐

B: I often remember what someone looked like but forget their name. ☐

C: I can't remember what people look like. ☐

10.

A: I often find myself humming or singing to the radio. ☐

B: I enjoy photography. ☐

C: I like to make things with my hands. ☐

11.

A: I would rather have an idea explained to me than read about it. ☐

B: I enjoy speakers more if they use visual aids. ☐

C: I like to participate in activities rather than watch. ☐

12.

A: I am a good listener ☐

B: I find myself evaluating others based on their appearance. ☐

C: I feel positive or negative toward others, sometimes without knowing why. ☐

13.

A: I can resolve problems more quickly when I talk out loud. ☐

B: I am good at finding my way using a map. ☐

C: I exercise because of the way I feel afterward. ☐

14.

A: I like a house with rooms that allow for quiet areas. ☐

B: It's important that my house is clean and tidy. ☐

C: I like a house that feels comfortable. ☐

15.

A: I like to try to imitate the way people talk. ☐

B: I make a list of things I need to do each day. ☐

C: I've been told that I'm well coordinated. ☐

Count the total number of A responses, B responses and C responses and note below.

A RESPONSES: _____

B RESPONSES: _____

C RESPONSES: _____

If you have more A responses your dominant mode is Auditory

If you have more B responses your dominant mode is Visual

If you have more C responses your dominant mode is Kinaesthetic

When you can define which communication mode is your prospect's dominant communication mode and can speak with them in that same communication mode, you are far more likely to be fully understood and obtain a buying decision. So how do you determine your prospect's dominant communication mode?

This is far easier than you might first imagine. You simply ask questions as you would normally do and listen carefully for the words and phrases that your prospect uses in their responses to you.

Prospects who are predominantly Auditory will use words and phrases such as:

'That *sounds* expensive'

'I haven't *heard* about that'

'That *rings* a bell'

'I *hear* what you are saying'

Does this Sound as if it is going to be easy for you to learn to do?

Prospects who are predominantly Visual will use words and phrases such as:

'I don't *see* what you mean'

'I hadn't *pictured* it quite like that'

'I can *see* your point of view'

'I need to *focus* on the bottom line'

Are you beginning to See how easy this is?

Prospects who are predominantly Kinaesthetic will use words and phrases such as:

'I don't *feel* it's for us'

'I think we can *firm up* an agreement'

'My *gut feeling* tells me…'

'I'm not *comfortable* with that'

Now do you FEEL you could pick this up easily?

Once you have established your prospect's dominant communication mode, here is how you adapt what you say and your presentation to communicate with them in the most effective way.

Communicating with an Auditory

If someone is dominantly Auditory, it is particularly important to mirror their rate, tone and pitch of speech.

When they ask you a question or make a statement and use an auditory word or phrase, you simply repeat it back to them and use other words that match their dominant communication mode. For example, if a prospect were to say to you "that sounds expensive", you would say "I appreciate that *sounds* expensive Mr Prospect, so may I just *talk* you through all the additional features that account for that price difference?"

If you need to use brochures, pictures, charts or any other form of visual support to illustrate your points, be very careful not to just pass that information across to them to look at. I'm sure that at some time when you have offered a prospect a chart or diagram, you have either seen a look of disinterest or they have brushed them aside and asked you to just explain your point. An auditory person needs to hear your information in words—not pictures. So talk them through what you are showing them.

Communicating with a Visual

When a visual dominant person asks you a question or makes a statement and uses a visual word or phrase, you repeat it back to them and use other words that match their dominant communication mode. For example, if a prospect were to say to you "I hadn't pictured it working quite like that", you would say "I *see* you hadn't *pictured* it working quite like that, so may I *show* you how this works and could solve that problem we discussed earlier?"

Unlike auditories, visual dominant people love to see pictures and diagrams that illustrate what you are explaining to them. So be armed with all the pictures, charts and diagrams you have available to you.

Communicating with a Kinaesthetic

Just as with the other two dominant communication modes, when a Kinaesthetic asks you a question or makes a statement and uses a kinaesthetic word or phrase, you repeat it back to them and use other words that match their dominant communication mode. For example, if a prospect were to say to you "I don't feel that would work for us", you would say "I understand you don't *feel* it would work for you. Would you allow me to loan you a demo model so you can *use* it and get a proper *feel* for how this could help you? I'm sure you will *love* it when you do."

Kinaesthetics love touching and using things and respond particularly well when you are demonstrative and emotional about your product or service.

At first read, matching communication modes may seem a rather more complex technique than any that we have covered so far in this book. Rest assured that once you start practicing them you will find them quite easy and very effective. Once you start to match your prospect's dominant communication mode, you will be sending a very strong message to their subconscious mind that you are just like them and it is OK for them to like you, trust you and do business with you. When you match your prospect's dominant communication mode, you are three times more likely to do business with them and therefore make it even easier to double your sales.

A Final Word — Power Words

I have already mentioned that the words 'please' and 'thank you' are two of the most powerful words we can use and the less they are used by others, the more powerful they become. There are also several other words that the advertising industry have identified as the most powerful words that can be used to motivate people into positive action. You will see these words used in powerful and effective direct sales advertisements, brochures, website promotions and all manner of marketing materials. They should be used in speech also. The words are:

DISCOVER   EASY   YOU/RE   LOVE   NEW

SAFE   FREE   INVEST/MENT   PROVEN   GOOD

OWN   SAVE   BEST   RESULTS   GUARANTEED

To illustrate my point, the following is a paragraph I have constructed which includes these words twenty-seven times. I appreciate you might think is more than just a little over the top, but it has been done to illustrate that it is possible to incorporate a lot of these words into a paragraph.

By INVESTING in this book YOU will DISCOVER how GOOD if feels to OWN and take control of YOUR life. YOU'LL LOVE the SAFE, PROVEN and EASY techniques YOU will learn many of which will be NEW to YOU. It is GUARANTEED to be the BEST INVESTMENT YOU have ever made and the RESULTS YOU achieve will make YOU and SAVE YOU a fortune in the future. YOU also get FREE access to my NEWsletter at www.bruceking.co.uk which is delivered direct to YOUR mailbox.

Study this list of Power Words and use them whenever you think it is appropriate to do so. Build them into your speech, your voicemail messages, your e-mails, brochures, web sites, reports and any other marketing materials you are using to help you achieve your goal to double your sales.

ACTION POINTS

When speaking with someone on the telephone, act as if you were really there in every respect

Mirror, Pace and Lead your prospects

Identify and communicate with your prospects in their Dominant Communication Mode

Use Power Words in all your communications

Continue with your PDP exercises daily

Do NOT move on to learning and applying anything in the next chapter. Just put into practice what you have learned this week and in previous weeks.

Chapter Six

Week Four

The Ultimate Selling System

*"The most important thing is not which system you use.
The most important thing is you have a system."*
Zig Ziglar

The Hard Sell And Consultative Selling

The days of the 'Hard Sell' are over! Or are they? The truth of the matter is that there are many, very successful companies in the market place who provide excellent products or services but still train their salespeople in the old fashioned, hard sell, foot in the door techniques. They have challenges recruiting salespeople to sell in this manner, but those whom they do attract and are successful, do make very substantial incomes. However, most salespeople prefer to work for companies that encourage a more low key approach to sales and have adopted a more 'consultative selling' approach to sales.

I have nothing against the consultative selling approach to sales. In fact one of my two favourite definitions of selling is:

Exposing companies or individuals to problems they never knew they had or opportunities they did not know existed, and showing them how your idea, product or service can help them solve the problems or exploit the opportunities, and getting them to buy.

The challenge with that definition is that many salespeople who adopt consultative selling techniques often forget the last four words in that definition, which are 'getting them to buy'. Indeed, it is my opinion that a lot of salespeople have simply gone soft on selling.

I remember very well when I was given my first ever business cards. I was so very proud to have them and sat and admired them for some time. It had the name and address of my company, my name, and underneath my name the single word 'Sales'. A few years later, whilst working with another company, my title was changed and my card bore the title Sales Executive. With the benefit of hindsight, it is quite obvious why the company changed my title. It gave me more prestige (not more money) and therefore made me feel better about myself. It also made the potential customer feel they were dealing with someone more important—an Executive rather than a Salesman. A few years later, and around the time that consultative selling became more fashionable, it became the norm for the title 'Sales Executive' to be replaced with the title 'Sales Consultant' —and that, in my opinion, was when the rot set in! Salespeople stopped selling and became consultants and, as you well know, salespeople do not get paid for consulting; we get paid for selling.

As I previously stated, I am totally in favour of the concept of consultative selling. I firmly believe that we must be focused on exploring our customers' needs and doing the very best for them we can. I believe that we must act with absolute honesty and integrity and that we must strive to build excellent and ongoing relationships with our customers. However, I also believe it is critical to our success that we never forget that we are selling, and it is my opinion that the hard sell just needs to be a lot more subtle than it used to be. Here is an example to illustrate this point.

A client of mine recently asked me if I could recommend a marketing consultant who could assist him on a short term, six month contract to develop a marketing campaign for a new product range he was launching. I believed I knew the right person and set up a meeting with the three of us so that I could introduce my client to Jonathan.

The important point to remember here is that my client hates to be sold to. I have seen him go into a frenzy at the slightest hint that somebody is trying to sell to him; it is not a pleasant sight and not a pleasant experience for the salesperson either. I also knew that Jonathan wanted this potentially very highly paid contract and, based on how I had seen him present himself in the past, I knew he was going to really sell himself to my client. It was going to be a very interesting meeting.

The three of us met a few days later. My client briefly outlined the project to Jonathan and then Jonathan took over. The meeting lasted ninety minutes and during that time I counted Jonathan asking thirty-nine subtle, well worded, closing questions that my client responded to every time. Not once did my client realise he was being closed on giving Jonathan the contract, step-by-step throughout the presentation. When Jonathan left, my client asked "Well Bruce, what do you think?" "What do YOU think?", I replied. He said, "It's good to meet with someone who's not in the least pushy, is very professional and can obviously do the job. So if you are in agreement, I'm going to hire him." The hard sell IS indeed just a lot more subtle now!

My second favourite definition of selling is:

Transferring you enthusiasm and passion for your idea, product or service to someone else and getting them to buy.

Note those last four words again!

A few years ago I was driving past a car showroom and noticed a brand-new, and very expensive, convertible sports car inside. With the hood down, it looked absolutely magnificent. Let me make it very clear that at the time I was most definitely not in the market for a new car, let alone one with that kind of price tag.

Nevertheless, purely out of interest, I parked my car and strolled into the showroom, just to take a closer look at this beautifully polished, white and chrome, dream on wheels.

You guessed it. I bought it. Or rather—I was sold it. That salesman was one of the best I have come across in a long time, and he knew it. Because he knew it, he really didn't come across as a salesman.

He didn't pounce on me and make me feel that I was being lined up to pay for his next holiday in the Bahamas. He was just confident, friendly and very eager to help.

Did he care about his product? I've never seen anyone care as much as this man did! He was immaculately dressed and carrying a very clean, nearly new, yellow duster. He noticed several 'invisible' finger-marks on the gleaming paintwork and delicately and lovingly polished them away while gently engaging me in conversation. He dusted tiny specks from the upholstery before I was eased into the driver's seat. He carefully wiped the leather steering-wheel before I got in, and polished the tiniest smear from the windscreen as I settled behind the wheel. All this was done quietly, discreetly and with absolutely genuine care for his product.

Did he care about me? You bet he did! He helped me off with my jacket so that it wouldn't crease when I sat in the driver's seat. He removed the price ticket from the windscreen so that I could get a perfect view of how that long, gleaming bonnet would look when I was driving it. He adjusted the seat for me, explained the controls quietly and with no hint of impatience and, when I was finally sitting comfortably admiring the deep-pile carpets and the magnificent dashboard, he told me how well I looked in the car, with the perfect choice of words.

Was he enthusiastic? It goes without saying. There wasn't a question he didn't answer as if it was more important to him than it was to me. He never criticized the competition, he only emphasised how much more I would love driving this car than any other, how I would be thrilled with its road-holding and comfort, how I would be delighted with its economical fuel consumption and how proud his company would be to look after the car for me when it needed any attention.

He also informed me that, by some amazing coincidence, a client of his was looking for the very car I was driving at the time and that he could therefore quote me a much better trade-in price for it. Of course, I never queried what the normal quote would have been. We had coffee in a quiet corner of the showroom and discussed the financing package but, by this time, it was merely a formality. I had been sold the car an hour ago and, even though I couldn't really afford it, I had to have it. I convinced myself that with a little extra sales effort on my part the purchase would not really cause me any financial problems. I still remember that salesperson to this day.

How many times have you gone out with the intention of buying something and walked out of a shop, store or showroom because the salesperson was unenthusiastic, boring or gave the impression that they simply did not care about you or their product? I have, many times. The price of the product was almost immaterial. I wanted someone to be as enthusiastic as I was about what I wanted to buy. Sometimes the salesperson has been so unenthusiastic that he or she has even put me off buying the product from anybody at all. Other times, I have paid a lot more than I need have done elsewhere, just because the person selling it was a great salesperson and even more enthusiastic than I was.

If you are not enthusiastic and passionate about your product or service, you have two choices; either find reasons to get enthusiastic and passionate about it, or leave and find something to sell that you can be passionate about. You are never going to be really successful in sales otherwise.

WHY PEOPLE BUY

People buy for emotional reasons and sometimes need logical reasons to justify their decision. Think about some your own buying decisions for a moment. Did you ever go out and buy a new pair of shoes when you had plenty already and your favourite pair just needed new heels, but you bought a new pair anyway because you just love new shoes? Maybe you justified your decision on the basis that if someone saw your bright, shiny, new shoes with the designer name tag, you would create a better impression. Did you ever buy a new car when there was nothing at all wrong with your current model, but the feel and smell of a new car really makes you feel good? Perhaps you justified your decision on the basis that a new, more expensive, luxury car would impress your clients and they would be more likely to do business with you.

I am sure you can think of lots of examples of when you bought something for emotional reasons and then justified them with a logical reason. My own little foible is that I always buy new socks to wear whenever I am speaking at a conference, seminar or workshop. I just love wearing new socks and my logical reason for spending hundreds, if not thousands of pounds a year on new socks, is because they make me feel so good I believe I will speak much better and therefore attract even more speaking work. I am also a little paranoid that if I do not wear new socks I may not feel so good and may not speak well, which leads me on to the next key point.

People buy for emotional reasons and sometimes need logical reasons to justify their decision and this applies equally in the business to business market as it does the business to consumer market.

The two fundamental emotional buying reasons are To Avoid Pain and To Be Happy. Which of those do you think is the greatest buying motivator? The answer is—To Avoid Pain.

I will use an analogy to demonstrate this point. Let us suppose that you wake up one morning feeling just a little depressed. You probably do not telephone the doctor, insist on an emergency appointment and demand a prescription for a 'happy pill'. There are many other ways you can cheer yourself up. You can go to a movie, go out for a drink or dinner with some friends, read an amusing book or just get on with the day and put up with a little bit of depression. You know that if you get on with your life the depression will probably soon lift and you will not need to be seeking out a therapist to help you with this.

Compare that situation to waking up one morning with a very bad pain in your head. You take a couple of painkillers but the pain does not go away and, in fact, it gets worse. A half-hour or so later it is so bad that you telephone the doctor for an emergency appointment. When you see them, you literally beg for a prescription for some drug that is going to take this pain away and seek reassurance that there is not something seriously wrong.

Pain is indeed the most powerful motivator, and so, wherever possible, we want to identify where a customer or potential customer is experiencing problems which are giving them pain. Once we have identified those painful situations and shown the customer how we can take the pain away, we are far less likely to get objections to what we are proposing and should have little or no difficulty in closing the sale. In fact the customer should almost be begging to do business with us.

At some workshops people challenge me and suggest that happiness can indeed be a motivator and that pain is not necessarily the most powerful of the two. On one occasion a delegate produced a list he had taken from another sales book, which showed the main motivational reasons why people buy. The following is that list:

- It is fashionable
- It looks good
- It is a status symbol
- It improves health
- It makes somebody love them
- It fulfils an ambition
- It provides security
- It makes life more comfortable
- It improves appearance
- It is enjoyable to own
- It will help to make more money
- It makes life easier
- It feels good

I went down the list with the group one item at a time and asked them these questions:

"Would somebody who was concerned about being fashionable be more likely to buy because something made them feel fashionable or because they were scared of being seen as unfashionable (PAIN)?"

"Would somebody who liked status symbols be more likely to buy because something was a status symbol, or because people would not feel they had any status if they did not have one (PAIN)?"

109

"Would somebody who was concerned about being loved be more likely to buy to make someone love them, or because if they did not buy it, they believed somebody would hate them (PAIN)?"

"Would somebody who was concerned about security be more likely to buy because they now had steel shutters on their windows which kept people out, or because they were petrified of being burgled or raped (PAIN)?"

I will leave you to complete the rest of that list if you wish to, as I did with those delegates. At the end there was not one who did not agree that from that point on, they would always focus on the PAIN.

Here is what I would like you to do next, and you may wish to do it right away or later in the day. It would be preferable to carry out this exercise with several of your colleagues so that you can brainstorm the answers.

Here are some very important facts which illustrate why this exercise is so important.

In the order of eighty-five percent of potential buyers are not looking for a solution to a problem. They either do not realise they have a problem, or they do realise it but do not believe there is a solution or a cost effective solution and have therefore decided to live with that problem. That is obviously a potentially enormous market.

The remaining fifteen percent who realise they have a problem and are looking for a solution are a much smaller market and, because they are already looking, will probably already be speaking to other companies who might provide the solution. So if you are prospecting for new business in this sector, you have a much smaller market and probably a lot of competition already.

It is therefore very obvious that you should be prospecting for new business in the 'don't know they have a problem' sector and, in order to do this effectively, you must have a list of questions you can ask that will enable your prospect to realise they have a problem.

I always believe in starting my approach to a prospective client as high up within the organisation as I can. I would far sooner get passed down to somebody with the introduction of the higher authority than get passed up by someone with a lower authority. By taking the 'top down' approach, I have the opportunity to ask that higher authority if they will need to be a part of the decision making process or if the person they are passing me down to has the authority to make a decision. The other important fact to recognise is that a known or unknown problem may be causing a completely different type of pain to different people within an organisation but for the same fundamental reason. Here is an example to illustrate this point.

Let us suppose that the XYZ Company has a problem, which is that its sales representatives are spending too much time with customers taking repeat orders that could easily be handled by a small tele-sales team, and as a result lack the time to prospect for new customers. As it is a large organisation, not everyone who might want to know or should want to know about this problem, may in fact know of it. However, the problem still exists and people at different levels within the organisation are going to be experiencing pain in a different way. I call this the Pain Ladder.

The CEO may be suffering pain because their shareholders are complaining about lower earnings per share and the share price has been falling. The reason for this is because profits have been falling.

The Director of Finance may be suffering pain because the profits have been falling. The reasons for this are increased operational costs of running the business, and new account revenue generation not meeting set targets.

The Director of Sales may be suffering pain because new account revenue generation is not meeting set targets. The reasons for this are that salespeople are spending too much time order taking with existing customers, and they are not opening sufficient new accounts.

You will note from the above that some of the pain is common to more than one category of person, wherever they are on the Pain Ladder, although because of their responsibilities, the reasons for their pain may be different.

Your first exercise is to compile a list of all the problems or painful issues that you have been able to identify for clients and potential clients and problems or painful issues they have told you about and asked if you could solve for them. Think long and hard about this and brainstorm it with your colleagues. It may also help to go over your file notes if you keep them. When you have a detailed list of every problem or painful issue you can possibly think of, compile a list of questions you could ask a potential customer or client that would get them to identify with that problem.

The next exercise, and another reason for involving your colleagues, is to gather a number of case references, and the more the better, that demonstrate to a potential client how you have solved various problems or pains for other people in other organisations. These are going to be extremely useful to help you all at various stages of the sales process.

Here is just one example of how a Case Reference should be written and is based upon the previous example of the Pain Ladder. This Case Reference could be used when first contacting a potential customer whom you believe may be suffering from a similar pain.

The Situation...
A particular situation that might be of interest to you concerned another Director of Sales of a major organisation in a similar field to your own.

The Issue...
Their salespeople were spending too much time order taking with existing customers and were not opening sufficient new accounts.

The Reasons...
Customers were required to place all orders, repeat or otherwise through the salesperson, leaving them insufficient time for developing new business.

We Identified...
Numerous methodologies that would be required to maximise the time a salesperson had to spend generating new business through prospecting and referral systems and ways to motivate them to achieve their targets for new business.

We Provided...
Assistance with developing the infrastructure and training required to achieve those aims.

The Results...
Over the following six months, the customer base increased by twenty-three percent and sales increased by nineteen percent.

Many companies I have consulted to have a section on their intranet detailing numerous Case References provided by the salespeople. This is particularly valuable for sales personnel who are new to the company. It is equally valuable to everyone who wants to be able to show or discuss a Case Reference relating to an issue specific to a prospect that they may not have in their own portfolio of Case References.

THE ULTIMATE SELLING SYSTEM

The system I am about to teach you is one I have been using and refining for many years. It breaks down into nine steps. Some of the headings may be familiar to you. The content may not be!

- Your initial contact
- Agreeing an agenda
- Getting an up front agreement to your terms
- Establishing authority
- Asking 'Facts Questions'
- Asking 'Issue Questions'
- Presenting your features and benefits
- Dealing with objections
- Closing the sale

Irrespective of whether you are selling a product or service which can be sold at the first meeting, or one that is a complex sale with a long selling cycle, the fundamental steps all apply. The fundamental difference in a complex sale will be that some steps may be weeks or months apart and may involve a lot more research and collaboration with others members in the sales team. Note that when I mention the words 'closing the sale' this applies equally to moving on to the next step in the sales process as it does to taking an order that day.

Your initial contact

Your initial contact with a prospect may be face to face, by letter, e-mail, telephone or, as is becoming more and more common nowadays, by voicemail. Your message, whether in writing or by voice, must be polite, to the point, highlight the potential benefits to the prospect of doing business with you (the WIIFM) and gain an agreement to move on to the next stage of the sales process.

If you are calling a referral—BEWARE! Do not assume that just because a prospect is a referral that you can be more relaxed or act in any way unprofessionally during your initial contact. At best, a referral will get you past the gatekeeper and will give the prospect a certain amount of trust in you. They may even return your call if you included in your message a reference to the referral—but that is all that you can expect.

The following is a version of what you could either write or speak in a more conversational manner. It is based upon the Case Reference structure and a referral to the prospect. You have asked for, and the referrer has given you, sufficient information about the prospect that you know what you are writing or saying is relevant. A bold headline is not necessary as you are mentioning an introducer in your first sentence. If this was an e-mail, the subject line would be 'Referral from Robert Smith' and would be CC to Robert.

Dear John

I am writing following my introduction to you by Robert Smith of The Board Company Limited.

Robert mentioned that a particular situation which concerned another Sales Director of a large organisation in a similar

114

business sector to your own, might be of interest to you.

The issue they had was that their salespeople were spending too much time taking orders from existing customers and were not opening enough new accounts. Customers were required to place all orders, including repeat business through the salesperson, leaving them insufficient time for developing new business.

We identified numerous ways to maximise the time a salesperson had to spend generating new business through prospecting and referral systems and ways to motivate them to achieve their targets for new business. We assisted them with developing the infrastructure and training required to achieve those aims and as a result, over the following six months, the customer base increased by twenty-three percent and sales increased by nineteen percent.

I would be delighted to meet with you and discuss this particular case in more detail and show you how we have helped many other organisations in similar fields to your own to increase their profits substantially. With this in mind I will telephone you within the next few days to arrange a mutually convenient appointment and trust this will be acceptable to you.

Yours sincerely

Conversational:

"Good morning John, it's Bruce King calling. I believe Robert Smith of The Board Company Limited told you to expect my call. Do you have a few moments right now or would you prefer I called you back at another time?"

(If OK, continue. If not—agree a specific time.)

"Thank you. Robert mentioned that a particular situation which concerned another Sales Director of a large organisation in a similar business sector to your own, might be of interest to you.

The issue they had was that their salespeople were spending too much time taking orders from existing customers and were not opening enough new accounts. Customers were required to place all orders, including repeat business through the salesperson, leaving them insufficient time for developing new business. Is that a situation you might also be experiencing?"

(Yes)

"Excellent. Thank you for confirming that. We identified numerous ways to maximise the time a salesperson had to spend generating new business through prospecting and referral systems and ways to motivate them to achieve their targets for new business. We assisted them with developing the infrastructure and training required to achieve those aims and as a result, over the following six months, the customer base increased by twenty-three percent and sales increased by nineteen percent. Would that kind of result impress you?"

(Yes)

"Thank you. What I would like to do is meet with you and discuss your situation in more detail and show you how we have helped many other organisations in similar fields to your own to increase their profits substantially. May we arrange that please?"

(Confirm date and time AND ASK FOR REFERRALS!)

If you have to leave an introductory message on voicemail, this should be based on a combination of the Introduction which I showed you in Week 2 and the above conversational script. For example:

"Good morning Mr Spens. It's Peter Jones here from the XYZ Limited, calling as suggested by Mary Applegate at Zone Enterprises. I believe Mary told you that I help large organisations manage their customer information to reduce customer turnover and drive repeat sales and suggested you

and I should meet up. Could you please give me a call back on 0845 113 1145? Thank you so much. I look forward to speaking with you."

SETTING AN AGENDA — YOUR FIRST MEETING

I am starting this section with another warning: If you do not have a selling system that puts you in control, then you are going to default to the buyer's 'buying system' and they are going to be in control. Which would you prefer?

Yes, buyers do have a system. Some buyers have developed their own system and others have been trained how to buy. In fact many buyers for larger corporations have more training in buying and negotiating than salespeople have in selling. However, I'm not referring to formal buying procedures here, I'm referring to four fundamental traits that most prospects you want to sell to have in common. These are:

1: Prospects know that a salesperson is meeting with them to sell to them and are therefore immediately defensive, even if they are a referral.

2: Prospects believe it is perfectly alright to lie to you and mislead you. Prospects who are generally totally honest and always act with integrity in almost every other situation, will have no qualms about lying to salespeople.

3: Prospects want to know what you know about the sector you are working in. They may ask for information about your customers and their competition and they want to know everything about your product and service and what it is doing for others. It is called unpaid consulting.

4: Having spent a considerable amount of time carrying out your unpaid consulting and producing sometimes complex reports and suggestions, prospects then think it is perfectly alright to ignore any of your follow up calls or other forms of correspondence. They will however, most graciously, give you unlimited access to their PA or voicemail.

117

Unless you have a selling system that overcomes most, if not all, of these traits, you are going to find it much harder to sell to them. Therefore, having established some immediate rapport as we described in Week 3, the next step is to set an agenda. The power of this process is that whilst you are asking questions which appear to the buyer to be giving them control, it is in fact you who are controlling the situation. You start with a question like:

"What are some of the things you would like to accomplish today John?"

OR

"John, when we spoke on the telephone last week and you agreed to meet, what was it that prompted you to invite me in? What are some of the things you would like to accomplish today?"

OR

"John, what was it about the letter and brochure I sent you that made you decide to call me in for a meeting? What are some of the things you would like to accomplish today?"

When they have finished explaining what their interest was and what they would like to accomplish, you then bring up the crucial points you would like to add into that agenda that are going to help you make the sale. You do this quite subtly by simply saying:

"Thank you, and what about (your crucial point 1)?"

"And what about (your crucial point 2)?"

"And would (your crucial point 3) be important to discuss?"

When you have all the points you want included, you summarize briefly all the points they have agreed need to be on the Agenda and move on to the next stage in the process.

Getting an up front agreement to your terms

Getting an up front agreement to doing business your way is an important step in the sales process for a number of reasons:

118

1: It shows the prospect that you are a professional person and expect to be respected, as they do.

2: It shows the prospect that you value your time and their time.

3: It is going to eliminate hearing those words that most salespeople dread to hear — "I want to think it over".

Here is how you gain that agreement. You say:

"John. I'd like to suggest we set some ground rules for this meeting. I assume you are going to want to ask me several questions about my company and our products and services, and how we might help you. I would like the opportunity to ask you some questions to make sure I fully understand your business and your concerns. Is that OK?"

The only answer they can give you is "yes".

"Thank you. As we go through that process, you might feel that our product/service is just not right for you. If that happens, rather than waste each other's time, are you OK with saying 'NO' to me please? You could say something like 'let's stop right now Bruce because I have no interest in this at all'. Are you OK with that?"

They have to agree with you. Who could resist the agreement and the opportunity to say "no" without hesitation?

"Thank you. On the other hand you may feel we have exactly what you want, in which case I'd expect you to say 'yes'. What I hope you won't say is 'I want to think it over'. I'd much rather you said 'NO'. Are you OK saying no to me John?"

Again you have given them the opportunity to say "NO'" which they will of course accept. And by agreeing to that, they have also agreed that they will not say "I want to think it over"!

Now you continue to the next stage of the sales process.

Establishing authority

At some stage in the sales process you may find out that the person you are presenting to is not the person who can make a decision. In a 'worst case scenario', and after making numerous failed attempts to contact your prospect after your initial presentation, you are going to realise that they had no authority to make a decision and, in fact, had been asked by a higher authority to get you to come in for some unpaid consulting. To avoid this, at some stage during the sales process you are going to need to find out if your prospect is the sole decision maker. To save what could be a great deal of your precious time, the sooner you find out the better! How do you do this?

You simply ask them! You say:

> *"John, in order to ensure I don't take up too much of your time and only give you relevant information, can you please tell me, if you really like what I have to show you, are you the only person involved in the decision making process or does anyone else need to be involved?"*

If they respond with the fact that they are the only person, you have your decision maker. If the answer is that others will be involved, here are some of the questions you must ask.

What are their names and titles? Their titles are particularly important for you to ascertain whether they are above or below the authority level of your prospect.

Will you get the opportunity to present to them as well? If the answer is 'yes', then you need to confirm what their particular interest will be. If that is on the agreed agenda to discuss, ask your prospect whether it is necessary to discuss it with your prospect or would it be better left to discuss with that other person.

If the answer is 'no', then you need to confirm their particular interests are represented on the agenda for you both to discuss. If not, get an agreement to add these and do so before continuing to the next stage of the sales process.

Facts questions

There are two reasons for asking Facts Questions and I shall deal with the most important first. I call it 'Painting the Picture'.

We salespeople often have the audacity or stupidity to assume that the moment that we start to speak with prospects, whether on the telephone or face to face, that they will automatically forget everything else that is going on in their personal and business lives and put themselves in the 'picture' that we want them to see themselves in. I will illustrate this using an example of how I might approach a prospect to whom I wanted to sell my sales training services.

- This is what I know about my prospect from my pre-call research:
- They are the Sales Director for the inbound telephone marketing division of a large finance corporation.
- The organisation has twelve offices countrywide.
- They have four hundred and fifty staff at each of their offices.
- They are advertising in national and regional newspapers every week for sales staff.
- Their profits have fallen by over fifteen percent in the last twelve months compared to the previous year.
- Their share price has fallen by six percent.

Now that is the picture I want them to be seeing from the moment I walk through their office door so that they can instantly tune in to my thinking and what I am going to present to them. Do you think they will be seeing that picture in their minds the moment I introduce myself? No, they will not! If that is the picture I want them to be seeing, I have to paint it for them. I do not approach this by telling them what I see and what I want them to see, but instead by asking Facts Questions. I ask questions that I already know the answer to so that they paint the picture for themselves and paint the picture I want them to see. I will ask:

- How many offices do you have?
- How many sales staff do you have at each office?
- How often do you have to recruit?

- How often do you lose staff?
- How much revenue do your average top salespeople—your A grades—bring in?
- How much revenue do your average B and C grades bring in?
- What is your budget for training?

I also ask some questions that I do not have the answer to but would like to know. That is the second reason for asking Facts Questions; to establish facts that I am not aware of but would like to know to complete my picture and their picture.

Note that these are Facts Questions and are not intended to disturb them. However, as I ask each question and they have to think about their answers, I have them seeing the picture in their minds that I want them to see and I am clarifying my own version of this picture. We are now thinking in tune. Now it is time to move on and expose the pain using Issue Questions.

Issue questions

Issue questions are formulated to expose known or unrealised pain. Following on from the previous example, here are some of the questions I could use to expose that pain.

- How difficult is it for you managing twelve offices?
- Is your advertising budget for recruiting a challenge?
- What issues do you face when staff leaves?
- How do you manage to train staff effectively when they are coming and going on such a regular basis?
- What is the impact of badly trained staff on sales?
- How many customers do you think you lose?
- How much is this problem costing you?
- Who takes a responsibility for a fall in sales?

Of course I do not ask these questions one after the other. As I ask each one and get a response from my prospect, we will have a discussion on each point before moving on to the next. You can, however, be sure that the prospect is hurting by now because I have exposed a lot of painful areas. I want them hurting a lot more and demonstrating extreme pain. How will you know when a

122

prospect is hurting sufficiently?

Prospects are only hurting sufficiently when they express feelings. Once you have exposed the pain with the above questions, you need to get the prospect to express feelings. To do this, you ask questions such as:

- How do you feel about that?
- How serious would you say that problem is?
- Do you find this frustrating?
- How angry does this make you?
- Do you get very upset about this?
- How much time do you spend worrying about this?
- Does your CEO give you a hard time over this?

When your prospect expresses strong feelings, you know they are really hurting. This is the time to present the features and benefits of your product or service and how it can take their pain away.

That is more than sufficient for this week. You have quite a lot of work to do preparing, learning, and putting into practice what we have covered in this section. When you have done that you will be well on the way to doubling your sales and we are only four weeks into the programme. Indeed, by the end of this week you may already have achieved your goal.

ACTION POINTS

Be aware whenever you are speaking to a prospect that you are there to sell—not consult

Be passionate and excited about your product and service at all times

Compile a list of all the problems or painful issues that you have been able to identify for clients and potential clients. Brainstorm this with your colleagues. Then compile a list of questions you could ask a prospect that would get them to identify with those problems and issues.

Again with your colleagues, prepare a number of Case References that demonstrate to a prospect how you have solved various problems or pains for other people in other organisations.

Prepare the basis of your initial contact letter and e-mail.

Prepare and learn precisely what you are going to say to a prospect when you leave a voicemail message and when you first speak with them

Learn the framework for setting an agenda

Learn the precise words for getting an up front agreement to your terms

Learn the precise words you will use to establish the prospect's authority

Identify and learn all the Facts Questions you can ask to paint your picture

Learn all the Issue Questions you can use to expose pain

Continue with your PDP exercises daily

Do NOT move on to learning and applying anything in the next chapter. Just put into practice what you have learned this week.

Chapter Seven

Week Five

Handling Objections

*"So many objections may be made to everything, that nothing can
overcome them but the necessity of doing something."*
Samuel Johnson

Examine that quotation above and you quickly see how it relates to
the importance of exposing pain. The more pain you can expose and
the more it hurts, the less likely a prospect is to raise objections.
However, human nature being what it is, you must expect to get
some objections from time to time and need to be prepared to deal
with them.

I have heard some sales trainers describe an objection as merely
a request for further information. Frankly, I think this is nonsense.
The dictionary definition of objection is 'an expression, statement
or feeling of opposition or dislike'. My thesaurus lists the following
words as suitable alternatives: censure, counter-argument, doubt,
exception, niggle, protest and opposition. How, therefore, could
anyone describe an objection as a request for further information?
That type of attitude to what is often a genuine initial rejection
of your proposals inevitably leads to failure to secure an order.
Fortunately, the psychology for handling objections is not difficult
to understand. However, before I move on to dealing with
the psychology of dealing with objections, let me illustrate the
importance of not giving in too easily.

Don't Give Up Too Soon

Mary was a salesperson for an office furniture supplies company. These scripts are taken from recordings of actual sales presentations Mary made before and after attending my How To Double Your Sales course.

Call One:

Prospect: John Smith speaking.

Mary: Good morning John. My name is Mary Wilson from Abbey Office Furniture. I understand you are the person who deals with purchasing office furniture. Is that correct?

Prospect: Yes but we don't need anything right now. Call me again in six months and I may discuss it then.

Mary: Thank you. I'll do that and I'm sorry to have troubled you. Goodbye.

Call Two:

Prospect: Robert James here.

Mary: Good morning Robert. My name is Mary Wilson from Abbey Office Furniture. I understand you are the person who deals with purchasing office furniture. Is that correct?

Prospect: Yes but we are quite happy with our current suppliers and the only reason we would ever consider a change is if you could offer us the same or a better product at a considerably lower price.

Mary: Thank you. Could you give me an example of something you purchase regularly and what you are currently paying?

Prospect: Just send me a catalogue of what you have to offer and your best prices and I'll take a look at it.

Mary: OK. Thank you, I'll put that in the post today and call you again later in the week.

Call Three:

Prospect: Susan Hart here. How can I help you?

Mary: Good morning Susan. My name is Mary Wilson from Abbey Office Furniture. I understand you are the person who deals with purchasing office furniture. Is that correct?

Prospect: Yes but I'm absolutely happy with my current suppliers and would not consider changing.

Mary: Not even if we were a lot cheaper than your current supplier?

Prospect: No. Thank you for calling. Goodbye.

This is how Mary dealt with similar objections after coming on my How To Double Your Sales course.

Prospect: John Smith speaking.

Mary: Good morning John. My name is Mary Wilson from Abbey Office Furniture. I understand you are the person who deals with purchasing office furniture. Is that correct?

Prospect: Yes but we don't need anything right now. Call me again in six months and I may discuss it then.

Mary: I understand and I appreciate your honesty. John, I'm calling because Abbey Office Furniture would like to be the company you look to when you do have a need for furniture. Our customers love our mix of quality, design and competitive pricing. Could you please tell me how we could position ourselves to earn the opportunity to be considered?

Prospect: Top of the list would be pricing. You'd have to be able to offer the most competitive prices. Why don't you just put a catalogue and price list in the post?

Mary: John, let's assume we could offer you the lowest or at very least most competitive pricing. What other factors would be strongly considered before you decided who you would place a future order with?

Prospect: Mary, just send me some information in the mail.

Mary: I'd be very happy to do that John. I have a tremendous amount of different literature here, some of which may not be of any interest to you. Do you mind if I ask you a few questions so I can just send what I believe will be relevant?

Prospect: Go on then.

Mary: Thank you. When do you anticipate you might need to invest in more furniture and is there a particular project you have in mind?

Prospect: We'll be fitting out a new tele-sales department for twenty operators in about nine months time.

At this point Mary asked a series of questions relating to the type of layout they were anticipating and the type of furniture required. Then:

Mary: John, I'm going to put some brochures together today. May I make an appointment to bring them round and go through the information with you? Can we organise that?

Prospect: No. Just put them in the post.

Mary: OK. I'll do that. How long do you need to review what I send you?

Prospect: Forty-eight hours I suppose.

Mary: OK, so I'll call you on Monday and here is what I would like to happen. If you are comfortable with this approach I'd like you to say that you have read through the brochures and particularly my notes on our free design service and there's absolutely no reason for us to meet. OR you can tell me that there is some interest, in which case I'd like you to call me in for a face to face meeting. Is that fair John?

Prospect: Very fair indeed Mary.

Mary: Thank you. You have a lovely week-end and we'll speak on Monday. Just one more thing before I hang up John.

I like to spend most of my time looking after my clients, not looking for them. So I'd really appreciate your help please. I believe there are several other offices on your business park and when I come to see you, I'd love to be able to drop in and introduce myself to two or three other organisations while I'm there. Who are your nearest neighbours?

Prospect: The only ones that spring to mind are Acme and Trident. You could call them.

Mary: Thanks for that. Would you by any chance know the names of the people I should be speaking to there?

Prospect: Joe Johnson at Acme but I don't know who at Trident.

Mary: Thank you so much for that. We'll speak on Monday. Goodbye.

Prospect: Goodbye. I look forward to your call.

Mary did make an appointment the following Monday, secured the order a few weeks later and has since transacted a substantial amount of business with that organisation. Mary did not give up as she had so easily in the past.

The Three Types Of Objections

The above conversation also illustrates the fact that there are three types of objections that prospects may raise. These are imagined objections, pretend objections and valid objections. Let us take a closer look at these.

Imagined Objections

The imagined objection is just that—a figment of your prospect's imagination. The following are typical examples of imagined objections:

- ◆ We couldn't afford it.
- ◆ I couldn't afford the running costs of this car; it's probably too heavy on fuel.

131

- I don't know if my wife would like it.
- I don't think it would fit.
- I don't think this carpet will match my curtains.
- I don't think I could get the board to agree

Now look at these statements again with my comments in brackets. It will be obvious that these are all imagined objections.

- We couldn't afford it.
  [Your prospect does not know the cost or what credit terms are available.]

- I couldn't afford the running costs of this car; it's probably too heavy on fuel.
  [They do not yet know that although the engine is larger, the new, improved fuel injection system increases fuel economy by 25 percent.]

- I don't know if my wife would like it.
  [He hasn't asked her yet.]

- I don't think it would fit.
  [She hasn't measured it yet.]

- I don't think this carpet will match my curtains.
  [He has not yet seen them together.]

- I don't think I could get the board to agree
  [He has not asked them yet.]

Pretend Objections

What about pretend objections? Probably the most frequent pretend objection you get is when a prospect claims to be too busy to see you. How many times has that been said to you? It is obviously a pretend objection. If I were to telephone you and told you that you had just won the Lottery, that I had a cheque for you for five million pounds and just needed fifteen minutes with you to complete the paperwork and give you the money, would you find the time in your very busy schedule to see me?

Other frequent pretend objections include:

132

- We cannot afford it
- It's not in the budget
- I don't have the authority to make the decision

Valid Objections

Valid objections are just what the title suggests. They are legitimate and real reasons why people may not be able to purchase your product or service from you and therefore are likely to be the most difficult to deal with. Nevertheless, you can deal with them on many occasions.

Having spent many years teaching thousands of people to sell a huge variety of products and services, it has become apparent to me it is very rare indeed that more than six valid objections can be made against any particular product or service.

It is essential to know all the imagined, pretend and valid objections that can be levelled against what you are selling, and to rehearse responses to them. This is therefore a further exercise for you to carry out, and as I often find that what one person in a company's sales force is finding difficulty dealing with, another finds very easy, this is again an exercise you should brainstorm with your colleagues.

THE BASIC RULES
FOR HANDLING OBJECTIONS

Before dealing with the basic rules for handling objections, I am going to introduce another concept which really falls under the heading of 'closing techniques', but which needs to be discussed now because you will use it frequently when handling objections.

The Silent Close

You will recall that I said right at the beginning of this six week programme that when I mention the term 'close the sale', it could equally refer to moving on to the next stage of the sales process as it could to getting an order. This close is most relevant now because when you are handling objections, you are in effect moving along a step in the sales process.

133

The golden rule is: **whenever you ask a closing question, keep quiet!** The first person to speak will almost certainly be the loser. If it is your prospect, he or she either has to say 'yes' to your proposition or raise another objection to going ahead. It will almost certainly be an objection that you can deal with. If you speak first, the pressure is off the prospect and back on you. You will have to spend a lot more time trying to regain control of the situation.

Charles was an ex-fighter pilot who had taken early retirement. He went to work for a company who specialized in leasing executive jets to large corporations and attended one of my training courses where he learned of the power of silence. Some months later he recounted this story to me.

Charles had been negotiating with the chairman and chief executive of a well-known public company for some weeks. The meetings had not gone as well as Charles had hoped but he managed to persuade them to take a trial flight in the jet he proposed to lease them. He hoped that a demonstration of the speed and efficiency of the service would convince them of its value to their company. He hired a chauffeur-driven limousine, collected the chairman and chief executive from their office and drove them to the private section of the airfield where they embarked for their trial flight.

His prospects were very quiet during the entire flight and, in spite of several probing questions, he could elicit little response. His prospects exchanged a few whispered words from time to time and made a few notes in their diaries. At the end of the flight they disembarked and got back into the limousine, which was waiting on the tarmac for them, for the journey back to their office.

Charles sat facing them in the rear of the car on the homeward journey and once again, although he made several attempts to strike up a conversation, his prospects remained silent throughout almost the entire journey.

As the car drew into the dimly lit underground car-park beneath his prospects' office Charles felt considerably less than confident. He was almost certain that once his prospects were out of the car he would never see them again. As the car drew to a halt, he made his move. "Gentlemen", he said, "in our earlier meetings, I believe I answered all your questions to your entire satisfaction. The trial flight that you have experienced has demonstrated beyond doubt that the efficiency and cost-effectiveness of this service would be of immense benefit to your company."

Charles then withdrew a contract and a pen from his inside jacket pocket, placed it on the small table between the seats and said: "If you would just sign this authority for us to proceed, we can have the jet ready for your use by the end of this week." He then sat back, smiled and kept quiet. Neither the chairman nor the chief executive smiled back. This took place at precisely 4.10 p.m. Sitting there in the silence of that dimly lit underground car-park, every minute seemed like an hour to Charles. At 4.22 p.m. the chairman picked up the contract and the pen, smiled and signed.

Charles earned more money in that twelve minutes of silence than he had earned in his last twelve months as a Royal Air Force pilot.

The next time you ask a prospect a closing question remember Charles. Keep quiet and you keep control—there is no close more powerful than The Silent Close.

Before dealing with common and specific objections, let us first take a look at the basic techniques for handling all objections.

1 — Respect Imagined And Pretend Objections

Earlier in the book we discussed the fact that people like to do business with people they like. Among the several attributes you must develop to become a top selling salesperson is the ability to make someone like you and to become their friend. Therefore, the most fundamental principle you must come to terms with when dealing with objections of any kind, is never to argue and never to let the experience of handling an objection develop into a confrontation. Whilst you may know that an objection is either imagined or pretend, you must always treat it as if it were valid. Nobody likes to be ignored or treated as if they were foolish and dealing with every type of objection as if it were a valid one will gain you the respect and friendship of your prospect.

2 – Acknowledge The Objection Before Responding

Whenever you are responding to an objection, always start by acknowledging it. It tells the prospect you have heard and accept what they have said. For example, when the prospect says to you, "It's more than we wanted to pay Bruce", you start your response with "I appreciate it's more than you wanted to pay Phil, and... (your response)."

Not only does this tell their conscious mind that you are listening, but because you are mirroring their speech, it is also telling their subconscious mind that you are just like them, they like you, can trust you and would like to do business with you.

3 – Listen And Let Them Finish

When I am presenting at a conference or workshop, I ask the attendees to raise their hands if they like to be interrupted when they are speaking. Not a single hand ever goes up. Then I ask how many of them interrupt other people when they are speaking. A sea of hands arises. Do you interrupt prospects when they are raising an objection or asking a question and taking rather a long time in doing so? I'll guess you do.

Why would you do this? You invest time in finding the prospect, researching their background, making the initial contact and securing an appointment. You invest time establishing a good rapport, asking facts questions, issue questions and then presenting how your product or service can help them solve their problems and remove their pain. You invest a lot of time and effort in your prospect. So why, when they raise an objection or ask a question, do you interrupt them and risk ruining the relationship and losing the sale when you were so close to getting the result you wanted. Nobody wants to do business with people who interrupt them.

From now on, no matter how many times you have heard the question or objection before, listen and let them finish. No matter how bored you are of hearing the same old thing time after time, you must look interested, nod, smile and let them know you are taking them seriously. Then use the 'Pause, Think, Respond' technique.

Even if you know the answer to it because you have heard the question many times before, do not immediately blurt the answer out. PAUSE and look as if you are taking the question very seriously and are THINKING about it. Whether it is an imagined, pretend or valid objection, your prospect needs to know you are taking it seriously. Then you can RESPOND.

4 – Ask Them To Elaborate

Sometimes prospects will have a genuine objection, but because they feel under pressure or are just not good at phrasing what they are thinking in a clear and concise manner, what they say is not necessarily what they mean. Ask them to elaborate, posing questions such as "I don't understand, can you explain that to me?" or "What do you mean exactly?" followed by the Silent Close.

Asking them to elaborate, rather than coming back with an immediate response, achieves a number of things.

- It gives them a little more time and takes the pressure off them
- It will give you a clearer understanding of their concern
- It makes them feel they are maybe a little smarter than you
- It makes them feel in control

That last point is particularly important. Whilst prospects want to deal with intelligent and professional people who are going to provide the highest quality of service to them, they can also be a little wary of people they think may be much smarter than they are. Asking them to elaborate therefore often makes them feel more comfortable with you.

The other major advantage in asking a prospect to elaborate on an objection is that in many cases he or she will talk themselves out of it without you having to say anything. This is particularly true of the imagined or pretend objection. Many times I have asked a prospect to elaborate and, after a lengthy silence and possibly some waffled explanation, they have agreed, without any prompting from me, that the objection was in fact invalid.

5 – Identify All The Real Objections

When a prospect feels under pressure or a little unsure, they will often stall the process by blurting out the first thing that comes to mind. If you respond promptly and satisfactorily to the first, they will just raise another. Therefore the technique you should use is to get all of the objections out in the open before responding to any of them. Very often it is only the last one that is, in fact, a genuine objection.

When the first objection is raised, you say: "Just supposing we could get around that" or, "Just supposing that wasn't an issue, is there anything else that is stopping you from going ahead?" (Silent Close).

If they raise another objection, you repeat that same question and keep doing that until all their objections are out in the open and they say "No—nothing else."

Then you ask, "So if I can satisfy you one hundred percent on each of those points, will you be going ahead?" (Silent Close). If the response to that is "No", you still have not got all of the objections out in the open and need to ask again "What else would be stopping you going ahead then?" If the answer is "Yes", only then do you answer the objections.

6 – Confirm They Are No Longer An Objection

Once you have answered an objection it is absolutely essential that you get your prospect's agreement that it no longer exists. Do not assume that because you have answered it to your satisfaction you have answered it to theirs. Ask "Have I covered that to your satisfaction?" (Silent Close), or "Are you now satisfied completely on that point?" (Silent Close), or "Is there anything else you need to know on that subject before I continue?" (Silent Close). Getting your prospect's confirmation that the objection no longer exists removes the likelihood of them raising it again when you are asking for the sale. An objection that has not been satisfactorily answered and confirmed as no longer relevant by your prospect, can always be brought up again.

Another useful technique you can use during this process, and one which is particularly effective when dealing with visually dominant prospects, is to write down in a list each of the objections raised. Write clearly and neatly and in full view of your prospect. As you deal with each objection and get their confirmation that it is no longer an issue, you draw a line through that objection. When you have got to the end of the list and every objection has a line through it, it is a very clear visual illustration to the prospect and a confirmation to their subconscious mind that they have no choice now but to keep their agreement to go ahead.

7 – Replace 'But' And 'However' With 'AND'

Having listened to thousands of salespeople answering objections, I know that you too often use the words 'but' and 'however'. For example, your prospects says to you, "It's more than we wanted to pay John" and you respond "'I appreciate it's more than you wanted to pay Phil BUT (or HOWEVER), let me run through the figures again and show you why it's going to give you such an excellent return on your investment."

Make no mistake about this, the words 'but' and 'however' are argumentative. They are a direct assault on the prospect's conscious and subconscious mind. You are effectively telling the prospect that they are wrong and you are right. On a conscious and subconscious level, you are raising a potentially insurmountable barrier between you and your prospect. You have possibly lost more business through using these words than anything else you could have done or said. In future, replace the words 'but' and 'however' with AND. Always remember that 'but' and 'however' separate people. The word 'AND' joins people together.

For example:

"It's more than we wanted to pay Bruce."

"I appreciate it's more than you wanted to pay Phil AND let me run through the figures again and show you why it's going to give you such an excellent return on your investment."

Do you see how much more effective this is going to be?

8 – Feel, Felt, Found

The feel, felt, found technique works so well with every prospect, and particularly with Kinaesthetics, that the best word to describe it is 'amazing'. This is an example of what you would say, tailored of course to your specific product or service.

> "I understand exactly how you FEEL (name). Many of our clients FELT exactly the same way when we first presented this solution to them. What they FOUND was that their return on investment was far better than they had expected and they have all become long term clients of ours"

Now look at the structure of that paragraph:

'I understand exactly how you FEEL'. This demonstrates that you empathise with their concern, that you understand them and are on their side.

'Many of our clients FELT exactly the same way...' demonstrates that it is quite alright for them to feel that way and that there is nothing unusual about how they feel.

"What they FOUND was..." demonstrates the benefits your other clients received as a result of their purchase.

Now let us take a look at some specific objections or stalls and the ones you are likely to come across most frequently.

PRICE OBJECTIONS

If there is one thing for certain that every prospect will try to negotiate on, it is price and price objections can be presented to you in a number of ways. A common statement voiced by a prospect will be "It's too expensive". Note I used the word 'statement'. They did not ask a question such as "How much can you reduce it by?", they just made a statement. Therefore even if you have the authority to reduce your price, this is not the time to start thinking about doing so.

The statement 'It's too expensive', should be responded to with a question from you, that should be either "Which means?" (Silent Close) or "So where do we go from here?" (Silent Close). In using either of these responses, you are passing the decision on what to do back to your prospect, which serves two purposes. Firstly, it makes them think they are in control because you have given them a choice and, secondly, and more importantly, it means they have to make the next move.

I used this technique with a prospect just a few weeks ago when I quoted them my highest price ever for a five day conference tour in India. When I asked (him) "So where do we go from here Ramin?" (Silent Close), I was met with a slight pause, followed by the response "I suppose we'll have to increase the ticket price a little then". Therefore, whenever you are faced with a price objection, do not automatically start thinking of reducing your price. There may be many other ways the prospect can meet your quoted price.

The prospect may come back with the same price objection, perhaps worded slightly differently such as in "It's definitely more than we want to spend". You could respond to this second price objection with the question "That's not unusual. Off the record, in round numbers, what price were you hoping for?" (Silent Close).

Of course it is not 'off the record', but a prospect's subconscious mind hears those words and associates them with genuinely being 'off the record'. This, combined with the words 'round numbers', puts the prospect off guard and they are then much more likely to tell you what they were actually hoping to pay, and are prepared to pay, than giving you a price way below as would often happen in a price negotiation. Another way of identifying what their price point is could be to ask the question: "In round numbers, off the record, how much too much is it?" (Silent Close).

Now let us take a specific example to illustrate how to deal with the response you may get from that last question. Let us suppose you are selling a piece of machinery at a cost of £150,000 and they have raised their second price objection. In response to your question "In round numbers Peter, off the record, how much too much is

141

it?", they say £15,000". Now you have two choices. You can either reduce the price or you can...

Focus On The Price Difference

I never want to reduce my prices without getting an equivalent financial benefit by re-structuring the deal. However, in this case, let us say that there is no margin to reduce the price and no restructuring possible. By focusing on the price difference of £15,000 you now have the prospect fixed on a much smaller sum of money than the total price you were first discussing. Here is how your presentation and response to this price objection should go now. You will probably need a calculator to hand so you can work out the precise figures easily as you work through the process.

> **You:** Let's look at the numbers Peter. This machine is going to last at least five years before it needs replacing. Agreed?
>
> **Prospect:** Yes.
>
> **You:** And you said you are open six days a week, forty-nine weeks a year, yes?
>
> **Prospect:** Yes.
>
> **You:** And the factory is operating two, seven hour a day shifts. That was correct wasn't it?
>
> **Prospect:** Yes.
>
> **You:** So this machine is going to be running and saving you money for at least fourteen hours a day, six days a week, forty-nine weeks a year for at least five years, which is twenty thousand, five hundred and eighty hours. And you said its fifteen thousand pounds too expensive. That works out at seven pounds an hour. Is seven pounds an hour really going to be an issue? (Silent Close).

If what you are proposing to your client is going to make financial sense, work out the figures on the above basis as they apply to your product or service, and take this approach of focusing on the price difference before ever thinking about restructuring the deal or reducing the price.

DEALING WITH —
'I HAVE TO DISCUSS IT WITH...'

Sometimes you may forget to establish early on in your presentation that the person you are speaking with has the authority to purchase. Other times, in spite of the fact that they had told you they do have the authority, they will still use the classic stall— "I have to discuss it with...." Now here is the challenge. They are either telling the truth or they are not, and you do not know which is correct.

If they had told you earlier that they had the authority to purchase then your response to this stall should simply be, "That is not what you told me earlier. Why have you changed your mind?" (Silent Close). Yes it may appear confrontational, but said quietly and pleasantly, it does not need to sound that way. They either told you a lie or they have changed the terms you agreed to, so you are perfectly entitled to ask that question and expect an answer.

If they had not told you that they had the authority because you forgot to ask, or they are adamant that in spite of the fact they had, they still have to discuss it with someone else, you then ask "Would you like to go ahead and will you be recommending you do?" (Silent Close).

If they seem unsure or say "No", then you have not sold them on your product or service. They still have concerns that need addressing and it is now up to you to start questioning again to identify the reasons why. When you have done that satisfactorily, you may well find that they no longer have to discuss it with anyone and that they were simply using that as an excuse because they were not convinced. If you had not asked that question, it is almost certain you would have lost the sale.

If, on the other hand, they say "Yes", then you need to ask a number of other questions. These could include:

"Would you like me to present our proposals with you?" This is, of course, the best option for you. (Silent Close).

"What help, information or other materials do you need from me in order to present this to them so they agree?" (Silent Close).

If they genuinely want to recommend they go ahead, you need to ensure as far as possible that they present your proposal in the best way available and have all the supporting materials required to do so.

DEALING WITH –
'I WANT TO THINK ABOUT IT'

It is estimated that when someone says they "want to think it over", in ninety-seven out of one hundred cases, they will not and you will not get the sale. Yes, you may get the remaining three out of the hundred, but with those odds I would far sooner you had a "no" and moved on to a new prospect than sat at home after a hard day's work believing you had all those prospects thinking your proposal over.

Last week I showed you how to establish the 'up front agreement', to avoid the prospect saying they want to think it over. Sometimes you will forget to set up the agreement and other times, in spite of the fact that they agreed, they may change their minds. If they have agreed not to think it over and still raise that objection, your response should be to say "That is not what we agreed" (Silent Close).

If you omitted to get an up front agreement, then this is the process you go through.

> **You:** I appreciate you may want to think about it. Generally speaking, when a client says something like that to me, it means I haven't explained something properly. So please tell me—what is it I've not made clear—is it the (name any one feature of your product or service that you think may have caused the objection e.g. cost/size/service intervals)? (Silent Close).

> **Prospect:** It's the cost of it.

144

You: I can understand that cost may be an issue. In addition to that, is there anything else that's stopping you from going ahead? (Silent Close).

Prospect: No.

You: So if we can deal satisfactorily with the investment required, is there any reason why we couldn't go ahead today? (Silent Close).

Prospect: No.

As I stated at the beginning of this chapter, the more pain you can expose and the more it hurts, the less likely a prospect is to raise objections. Nevertheless, objections will come up from time to time and the more effectively you can handle them using these techniques, the easier it will become to double your sales.

ACTION POINTS

Brainstorm with your colleagues all the valid objections that can be raised to your product or service and have appropriate responses prepared.

Learn and put into practice all the basic rules for handling objections

Learn and put into practice the way to deal with price objections

Learn and put into practice the process for dealing with price objections

Learn and put into practice the process for dealing with 'I have to discus it with...'

Learn and put into practice the process for dealing with 'I want to think about it'

Continue with your PDP exercises daily

Do NOT move on to learning and applying anything in the next chapter. Just put into practice what you have learned this week and in previous weeks.

Chapter Eight

Week Six

Closing The Sale

"Always be closing. That doesn't mean you're always
closing the deal, but it does mean that you are always
closing on the next step in the process."
Shane Gibson

I hear a lot of sales trainers and salespeople complain about
the use of the term 'closing a sale'. One of the criticisms often
voiced is that the word 'close' relates to the end of something,
whereas getting a sale from a customer should be the 'start' of a
relationship. Others feel it is too harsh a word and reflects badly on
their professionalism. Well I say 'phooey'!

The term 'close the sale' is brief, to the point, and we all know what
it means. It means getting an order or an agreement to move on to
the next stage in the buying process. Selling is the oldest profession
and the term 'close the sale' has been used for hundreds of years
and will probably be used for many hundreds more to come. This
chapter is all about 'closing the sale'.

If You Don't Ask For The Order — You Won't Get It

Salespeople don't plan to fail but they often fail to close. This point
was vividly illustrated to me some years ago by a shower salesman.
My family and I had just moved to a very expensive neighbourhood.
We had chosen a slightly smaller house than we really needed

because of the high prices in the area and we decided to install a shower-room to ease the morning queue outside the bathroom.

A representative from a well-known company visited us late one afternoon. He was very presentable and knew his product well. I was impressed. He spent the first half an hour running through the various models that were available and the technical specifications of each. I mentally decided on the most appropriate one for our needs. After a tour of inspection of the house, and after taking measurements in various rooms, the most appropriate site in which to install the equipment soon became very apparent. Over a cup of coffee we ran through the technical specifications of the model I had already set my mind on and the costs of supply, delivery and installation. I was ready to sign the order. At this point, the super-salesman thanked us for our time and patience, placed a quotation and some literature on our coffee-table, and got up and left. His parting words were, "I'll wait to hear from you then."

I was totally flabbergasted. I wanted the equipment. I wanted to buy it from his company and I was ready to sign an order form immediately, but he did not ask me to. His lack of enthusiasm or his fear of closing the sale rubbed off on me. The following day over breakfast my wife and I decided that we could probably do without the equipment anyway as it was very likely that we would be moving on again in a year or so.

You may think this is an extreme example but I can assure you that thousands of times every day, in every country throughout the world, a salesperson fails to ask for the order. Even when there is an obviously willing buyer and where the sale is there for the asking, the same rule applies. If you don't ask for it—you probably won't get it! Customers need help in making a buying decision. They find it hard to ask to buy and it is your responsibility to make it as easy as possible for them to do so.

In spite of that, the thought of closing the sale still seems to strike such terror into the hearts and minds of even the most experienced and competent salespeople. If it is the right prospect with the need and the means to buy, if the presentation has run smoothly and objections, if any, have been handled successfully, asking for the order should be the natural and obvious next step. So often it just does not happen. The target you have set for yourself is to double you sales in just six weeks. If you do not ask for the business during and at the end of your presentation you are not going to achieve that, so I am going to share thirteen of the best closing techniques that I know.

THIRTEEN OF THE BEST
CLOSING TECHNIQUES

The fact of the matter is that at least ninety percent of the time when I am selling I only use number one, two and thirteen, and you could do the same and still double your sales. So why have I included eleven others?

There are two reasons for giving you these thirteen closes. Firstly, they all work very well in many situations and it is good for you to know them all, even if you choose not to use them. The other reason is based on the fact that if we believe something will work for us, then it will and if we believe something will not work for us, then it will not.

You may read through and study these thirteen closes and believe that others will work better for you than the three I use most frequently. If that is the case, use them—because you are right!

1 — Get The Prospect To Close The Sale

This close is the easiest close, the least stressful to both the salesperson and the prospect, and if you just used this close and only this one, you would double your sales. Here is what you say after you have exposed all the pain you can and presented the features and benefits of your product or service and how they can solve the pain.

You: John, are you now one hundred percent certain that what I have to offer can solve those problems?

Prospect: Yes.

149

You: In that case, what would you like me to do now? (Silent Close) OR So what happens next? (Silent Close).

You have taken all the pressure off yourself but you have not put any pressure on the prospect. You have not asked them for the business; you have given them a choice. Of course the only sensible choice they can make is the one you want.

2 – Asking For The Money

Getting an agreement on the pricing is another method for closing a sale. Now I know that many salespeople do not like asking for money, or even talking about money, and when the time comes the salesperson begins to get a little panicky and the easy flow of the presentation starts to stall.

Providing you have exposed sufficient pain and the prospect seems eager to deal with it, why should you have a problem asking for the money? Your prospect certainly was not expecting the solution to come without a cost and opening up the discussion on it as early as possible can also enable a prompt close. Therefore you can simply say, "The investment required to solve these problems is going to be in the region of (£XXX). Is that going to be OK with you?" (Silent Close). If they respond with a "Yes", you have made a sale.

If you have a variety of solutions to their pain, each with a different price point, you could deal with the price in a number of ways. For example:

You: Do you have a budget available to solve these problems?

Prospect: Yes.

You: Would you mind sharing that with me in round numbers? (Silent Close).

OR

You: Do you have a budget available to solve these problems?

Prospect: No.

You: How are you planning to pay for the solution then? (Silent Close).

Prospect: Well how much is it going to cost me?

You: As you can imagine, there's a number of ways we could solve these problems. Some solutions run from between £5,000 to £10,000, others from £11,000 to £19,000 and sometimes we'll tailor packages at £20,000—which of those price brackets do you think you'd be looking to work in?

The most important point I want you to be aware of is that it is OK to discuss money. If you hesitate, your prospect's subconscious mind will pick up on this and they will inevitably put pressure on you to reduce the final price because they know you do not like to discuss it and that you will be likely to agree, just to get it over with.

3 — Start With A Close

Salespeople who attend my courses often ask me when they should start closing. My answer is very simple. You are starting to close from the moment that you start to speak. When you ask for the business it is just your final closing question.

If you are selling a product or service which can be closed in just one sales call, you can shorten the entire procedure and reverse the normal sales process by starting with a close. For example:

Salesperson to a couple who have just walked in to a bed showroom (it could be any other type of showroom): "Good afternoon. Have you come here to buy a bed today?"

Salesperson selling office supplies calling on a customer for the first time: "Good morning Mr Smith. Have you invited me in to place a first order with us today?"

Asking a closing question right at the beginning of your conversation is a very powerful technique. When you ask that question, your prospect's subconscious mind is involved in the response and knows that they do really want and possibly have a need to purchase what you are selling.

4 – The 'Confucius Close'

I mentioned the power of the silent close earlier and have been repeatedly noting throughout the last two chapters where you should be using it.

The longest period of time I ever sat in silence with a prospect after asking a closing question was twenty-seven minutes! My prospect knew the silent close and after about thirty seconds of me sitting there silently and smiling, he broke into a broad grin. I knew he knew, and he knew I knew he knew. This was going to be a test of wills and for twenty-seven minutes we just sat there grinning at each other, sometimes having to force ourselves to stop giggling. Then I used the 'Confucius Close'—one close he did not know.

The 'Confucius Close' is simply a way of bringing the silence to an end, hopefully without losing. After a few minutes silence, or as much as you can take or have the patience for, turn to your prospect and say: 'Confucius say, silence means agreement.' This must be said quietly, with extreme confidence and with a genuine smile.

5 – Turning A Question Into A Sale

This is another very powerful closing technique and there are frequent opportunities to use it during many sales presentations. How can you turn a question from a prospect into a close? Let us look at a few examples:

Prospect: Does it come in red?

You: Would you like it in red?

Prospect: Yes. [They have bought it]

Prospect: Is there a diesel version?

Salesperson: Would you like a diesel version?

Prospect: Yes. [They have bought it]

Prospect: Can I pay for this monthly?

Salesperson: Would you like to pay for it monthly?

Prospect: Yes. [They have bought it]

Turning a question into a sale will work wonders for your closing ratios and, with practice, can be introduced many times into any presentation. It can also be sharpened up and extended, depending on the type of question you are asked. For example:

Prospect: Is this model available in a diesel version?

Salesperson: Would you like it in a diesel version?

Prospect: Possibly. Would it be available by the end of next week?

Salesperson: If I can get it to you by then, can you approve the order today?

Prospect: Yes. [They've bought it]

6 — The Balance Sheet Close

The Balance Sheet Close is particularly useful with all analytical buyers and with procrastinators, timid and grumpy buyers, whether they are analytical or conceptual.

They all tend to have difficulty in raising objections and find it just as difficult to make decisions. The Balance Sheet Close is an excellent way of forcing a decision.

If you are going to use this type of close it is very important that you practice it over and over again until you become fluent and professional in your presentation. This is how you take the prospect through the closing process.

You: I appreciate how difficult it can sometimes be to make a decision. Many people, and particularly those in more senior positions, have so much on their minds that they have developed a decision-making procedure which saves them a lot of time and, ultimately, a lot of money. This was demonstrated to me some years ago, Mr Prospect, by the chairman of a major public company, who informed me that as a result of using this formula he had saved and made his company many millions of pounds. I am sure this will be very helpful to you with our current situation. May I explain to you what we need to do?

Prospect: Yes please.

You: We will take this large sheet of paper, Mr Prospect, and divide it into two columns. On the left-hand side we will head the column 'Reasons for going ahead now'. (Take the emphasis off the word 'now' as you speak it but make sure that you write it in slightly larger letters.). At the top of the other column we will write 'Reasons for not going ahead now'. (This time you emphasise the word 'not'.)

The next thing we do is to put down all of the reasons for making a positive decision in this left-hand column and then the reasons against in the right-hand column. When we have finished, if there is a significant difference between the numbers in either of the two columns, then the decision will be made for us. Are you OK with that?

Prospect: Yes.

You: Mr Prospect, what are some of the positive points, reasons to go ahead NOW, that we have discussed so far?

From now on you prompt your prospect as much as possible, give him suggestions and write in the left-hand column as many definite reasons for going ahead as you possibly can. If you have prepared yourself thoroughly beforehand you should be able to get down at least thirty to forty good reasons why your prospect should go ahead with the purchase. When you have done this, push the piece of paper across to your prospect, hand over your pen and ask him to write in the right-hand column as many reasons as he can for not going ahead now. The difference is that this time you offer him very little help whatsoever.

I have never yet met a prospect who managed to get down more than four or five reasons against going ahead with my proposals when faced with the Balance Sheet Close. When your prospect has finished writing, or when you see that he is having a problem, simply lean across the desk or table, look at the sheet, look him in the eyes and say: "Mr Prospect, that seems to have made our decision for us, doesn't it?"

7 – The 'Maybe You Cannot Afford It' Close

This close is only to be used with the snob and the dealer, whether analytical or conceptual. It appeals to their most basic instinct— their sense of pride. To make this close work successfully you need to be very casual, slightly subservient and almost apologetic. An outright challenge would work entirely against you.

The Maybe You Cannot Afford It Close can be used whenever you are selling more than one of a particular item and where superior and more expensive versions of your products are available. It can also be used for any service that can be offered at different levels, at different costs and for any programme or system where installation is normally carried out over a period of time in order to spread the cost for the client.

A real estate developer in California who learned this technique from me used it very successfully when a development of one hundred and forty two condominiums that he had up for sale along the coast were not selling too well. I suggested that he might promote them as investments for holiday rentals, as opposed to permanent homes, and the market at the time seemed right to take this suggestion forward.

A typical Mr Snob visited the development sales office one morning and my client informed him that, although units were available singly, there were substantial discounts on multiples of five or more. In a soft voice he added the words, "although I don't suppose that's within your budget, is it?" This was said very politely, slightly apologetically and Mr Snob rose to the bait. "Of course I can afford five units—where do I sign?"

I know several financial planners who have used this close on many occasions with great success. In preparing a financial planning programme for a potential client it is quite common to put together one which, under normal circumstances, would be put into place over a two-to-four-year period.

A Mr Snob or a Mr Dealer can be persuaded to put the entire programme into place immediately. This is one example of how to phrase your proposal:

> *"I have put these proposals together for you and I am sure you will find them very interesting. They will help you to achieve precisely the objectives you have given to me. However, in view of the complexity and cost, I don't suppose that you will be able to afford to effect all the contracts today. Therefore, I think we need to look at a planned process of installation over, say, the next two to three years."*

Mr Snob or Mr Dealer will often rise to the bait and implement all the proposals in the plan immediately. Without this covertly challenging approach they will inevitably settle on the two-to-three-year plan. On the basis of the challenge to his subconscious mind, all the transactions will invariably be carried out immediately.

Whenever you come across a Mr Snob or a Mr Dealer, think of the 'Maybe You Cannot Afford It Close'.

8 – The Invented Deadline Close

The Invented Deadline Close does not necessarily have to be invented and, in fact, I prefer that you did not. I firmly believe that acting without integrity attracts people who will act without integrity towards you. Nevertheless, I mention it because it is used frequently by many companies to encourage people to swiftly sign on the dotted line. Even if you do not use them, at least you will have been forewarned as to what you could expect when somebody is selling to you.

There will often be times when you have a limited number of end-of-range products, or when you are offering a discount on a service because your company is going through a particularly quiet patch.

If there is no official deadline, but limited availability, you can always invent one.

The financial planning industry is fortunate in respect of genuine deadlines. Frequent changes in taxation and legislation, anticipated changes prior to the announcement of annual Budget strategies or local or national government elections, give financial services salespeople countless openings to present prospects or clients with deadlines that could provide opportunities to save, or make money if they act quickly.

Here are some examples of deadline closes that have been presented to me. I have no idea if they were invented or genuine:

> "Mr King, we currently have a CRM programme which is being used by some of the major corporations in the country. These have been installed only quite recently and, according to our information, these will be satisfactory for these very companies for at least ten to fifteen years. However, we recently hired a team of programmers to develop a new system for us which, frankly, I do not believe is a good decision by our CEO. The costs of this new CRM programme are likely to be at least double that of our existing version. We can only offer the current one for another thirty days and have limited capacity to supervise the installation, so if you are looking to save a considerable sum of money, I'd suggest you invest in this system right now."

AND

> "Mr King, I have inside information from the sales department at the manufacturers that this model is soon to be replaced by the updated version, which is going to cost some £5,000 more. I also happen to know that the increased cost is not justified as the improvements are very minor. However, we will be committed to taking this stock, as will all other dealers, and we are therefore prepared to offer you one of the last few of this model, and with an additional five percent discount."

This type of close is nothing more than a sophisticated version of 'The Last One' close used by so many retailers. Probably the classic example of this is when my wife is being sold a very expensive dress or coat in a store. If she is showing more than the slightest interest the salesperson will probably say: "Before you get too enthusiastic about this particular style, I had better check in the storeroom and see if we have your size. This is a very limited edition and has been very popular." Of course, she returns a few minutes later with the information that there is only one left. My wife usually buys it, although I suspect there is usually a whole rack of her size in the store room. Of course, I've never told her that.

9 — The Assumptive And Secondary Question Close

Use this close when you are fairly certain that your prospect is willing to accept your proposition and all that is necessary is to put it to bed quickly. The technique is based on posing the major buying question first, then immediately by-passing it with another question of lesser importance which is much easier to make a decision on than the main purchase. Here are a few examples:

Salesman: I think we have covered everything now Mr Prospect. We just need to complete the order form. By the way, will you be arranging your own insurance, or would you like us to arrange this for you?

Prospect: I will be arranging my own insurance, thank you. [They've bought it]

Salesperson: From what we have discussed so far Mr Prospect, I think the computer with 1000 gigabytes is going to be most suitable for you. Would you prefer it in black or silver?

Prospect: I would prefer black. [They've bought it]

Salesperson: From what we've discussed, the Bahamas seems to be the ideal holiday for you and your family. Will you be paying by cheque or credit card?

Prospect: By credit card. [They've bought it]

The psychology behind this type of close is very simple. As I stated previously, it is the salesperson's responsibility to make the close as easy and painless for the prospect as possible. Giving them the opportunity to agree to some very minor point means that the major decision, and the most expensive one, is taken out of the picture completely. Buyer resistance vanishes with this style of close.

10 – The Weak Spot Close

Some years ago I was involved with a house-building company in Scotland. We had built a number of small, luxury holiday homes on a lake-shore site. They had the most magnificent views but, due to cost constraints, the rooms had been kept to a minimal size and we had not been able to use the highest standards of fixtures and fittings as we would have wished. Nevertheless, the homes were selling reasonably well, although not nearly as fast as we had hoped.

One bright afternoon I was showing a prospective purchaser and his wife around the development and was keen to sell the house in which they had expressed some slight interest. It was one of the first to be built and had been on our hands a long time.

The very first thing my prospect's wife said when she walked into the kitchen was: "Oh, what a wonderful view. I was brought up in a home overlooking a lake and I have always wanted to live somewhere like this again." This was her weak spot. We then moved into the living-room. The husband expressed concern at its dimensions. I immediately pointed out the open fireplace and the wonderful view across the lake. We then moved upstairs into the first bedroom. The same sequence of events took place there and in the other two bedrooms. In each case the husband expressed concern at the size of the rooms and also commented on the quality of the fixtures and fittings. I agreed, and pointed out the wonderful view across the lake from each bedroom.

Although I was talking to the husband most of the time, I was really selling to the wife. It came as no surprise to me that, after a few minutes by themselves in their car, they returned and made me an offer. I refused this and stuck out for the full asking price. "Is there anywhere else with a view across a lake quite like this?" I asked. They bought the house at the full market price.

Look out for a prospect's weak spots. They occur in almost every type of market and with almost every type of buyer. Whenever an objection is raised, answer it and then remind your prospect of that single feature that is so very attractive to them.

11 — The Take It Home And Try It Close

This close almost never fails and I believe the first person to use this technique was a pet shop owner in California. He used to get so many people visiting his pet shop who loved looking at the puppies and playing with them, but only a very few ever bought them. Then he came up with a cunning plan.

As soon as a parent with children came into the store and started looking at the puppies, he would approach them and say, "Sir (or Madam), you really shouldn't even think about buying a puppy today. Sometimes they get on famously with a new owner and sometimes it can be a real disaster. Sometimes they get on great with kids like yours and sometimes they don't. Tell you what I'll do though. I'll let you take this little fella home for a few days and you can see if he fits in and gets on with everybody. If he doesn't you just bring him back. Would you like to do that?"

The kids would scream "Mummy, mummy—can we do that please!" and mummy could hardly ever say no. Nor could she ever bring the puppy back again.

The same technique has been used to sell automobiles, televisions and other electronic products, paintings and a host of other goods. Once the children have used them, or the neighbours have seen them, it's very hard to send them back.

If a product is expensive and you stand to make a good profit on selling it, let your prospect use it. The cost to you of the rare damaged return will be far outweighed by the money you earn on products that never come back. If you have got it and can spare it—lend it.

12 – The Blank Order Form Close

Almost every product or service requires an order form or authority for your prospect to sign. If you do not have one, design one.

Without making it too obvious, try and make sure that your order form is in front of you, and in view of your prospect, either at the start of your presentation or some time during it when you produce reference literature or testimonials. At some stage, when you feel your prospect is ready to be closed, ask for a piece of information that you require to fulfil their order and write it on the form. It could be your prospect's full name, their company's name or address, or information relating to one of the products or services you are selling.

The moment your prospect sees you write something on your blank order form and does not question it, you know they have bought. The rest of the sales process is a mere formality.

In some sales situations it can be appropriate to enter the company's name and address on the form even before you get into the meeting. By leaving this in full view of your prospect, with his or her name and address at the top in bold capital letters, you are sending a very clear message to their subconscious mind that you expect a sale.

13 – The Door Knob Close

I have used the Doorknob Close all of my selling career and I estimate that it has increased my sales by at least ten percent over that time. That equates to a lot of money.

You use the Doorknob Close when you have tried everything you can possibly do to make a sale and there is nothing left but to quit.

You pack your briefcase, rise from your chair, thank your prospect warmly for seeing you and giving you the opportunity to demonstrate your product or service to them. As you get to the door, you push or pull it half open, and keeping your hand on the door knob, you half turn around and make the following statement:

You: Mr Prospect, just before I go, may I please take my sales hat off and ask you one more question?'

Prospect: OK then.

You: I hope you don't mind me asking but, as I am sure you are aware, I make my living selling this particular product. I thought I had presented it to you properly. I felt you had the need for it and that I had demonstrated the benefits to you accurately. I was quite certain that you would want to buy it. Just so that I don't make the same mistake again, could you please tell me where I went wrong?

The door is still half open, your prospect thinks you are leaving and is off the hook and relaxed. With your salesperson's hat off, they are even sympathetic and eager to help. They finally give you the real reason. Then it is up to you to get back in the chair and deal with that final objection. It takes a little bit of nerve, but it is worth the effort.

This is the last week of your six week programme and with so many effective closes now available to you, how can you possibly fail to double your income? Your subconscious is already totally convinced. Closing the sale after a good presentation has never been difficult. Using these techniques it will become even easier.

ACTION POINTS

Study the thirteen closes and select just a few that you believe will be the most useful to you—and learn them.

Continue with your PDP exercises daily

Do NOT move on to learning and applying anything in the next chapter. Just put into practice what you have learned this week and in previous weeks.

Chapter Nine

Moving on with PDP

"Imagination is everything.
It is the preview of life's coming attractions."
Albert Einstein

Most salespeople are in a hurry. We want results and we want them fast. What I have shown you in this six week programme are the techniques I have taught to tens of thousands of people in several different countries, many of whom have gone on to double their sales or increased them still more. Those that have achieved this did so because they followed the programme precisely as it should be followed.

Those of you who have followed this six-week programme religiously will have almost certainly doubled their sales or be well on their way to doing so and you should congratulate yourselves. Thinking back over what you have achieved since starting the programme should make you want to carry on working on your sales techniques, and working on yourself as I describe later in this chapter.

I also know that many readers will have hurried through this book, as they have been through so many others, sought out what they considered to be the nuggets that they believed would help them, and not followed the programme at all. Nevertheless, you will have learned techniques that will have helped you increase your sales significantly.

If you are one of those people, I urge you to go back and start again. If you follow this programme through as it was intended to be, you will never need to read another sales book again. You have everything you will ever need contained within these pages to achieve anything and everything you want from your career in sales.

MORE PDP EXERCISES

For the first six weeks of your programme, you have used PDP exercises solely to programme your subconscious mind to double your sales, and if you have been doing this persistently as I asked you to do, then you have almost certainly achieved that goal. Now you can stop that particular exercise and start to use PDP exercises to improve other aspects of your personality and behaviour in ways that can enable you to achieve even more in your sales career. Then you can move on to use these techniques to enable you to achieve anything and everything else you want from life.

WHAT MAKES A GREAT SALESPERSON?

These are the attributes that make a great salesperson:

Positive thinking

There is no other profession in which rejection is so likely to occur and where the ability to think positively is therefore so vital.

A great sense of pride in what you do

Salespeople are often maligned by the public and the media and are frequently the subject of cruel jokes. Some salespeople are even ashamed to admit they sell for a living. Do not ever forget that without salespeople almost every other form of employment would cease.

Practically everything that is made has to be sold.

Self-motivation

Average salespeople get average support from their colleagues. Top salespeople people also get average support and possibly less. To be better than average, you cannot rely on others to motivate you. You must know what you want and have the self-motivation to go and get it.

**The ability to get on with all types of
people and develop relationships quickly and easily**

This is vital. People like to do business with people they like, trust
and enjoy doing business with.

An open mind

If you really want to succeed, you must be prepared to do anything
that will always keep you a little bit ahead of your strongest
competition. You need to be open minded to anything that could
improve your performance.

Confidence

You must be confident in your abilities and never doubt that you
can achieve anything you want.

Fearlessness

Fear can be the downfall of otherwise excellent salespeople. The
sales process has many stages to it and some of the activities
involved in the process may scare you and cause you to hesitate
to do them.

Which of these are your weakest points and which are the strongest?
Take a blank sheet of paper and divide it into two columns. On the
top of the first column write 'My Strongest Attributes' and on the
top of the second column write 'My Weakest Attributes'.

Go through the list and with total honesty and taking as long as
you need, allocate the attributes I listed to one or other of those
columns. When you have done that, write down anything else you
believe may be holding you back from achieving your greatest
potential.

The following example by a salesperson I was mentoring will give
you an idea of what this could look like.

My strong points

- Positive thinking
- Confidence

- I am very proud of what I do
- I get on well with all types of people and make friends easily
- Open minded

My weak points

- I am not always self motivated and I often blame external factors for failure to reach my targets. I often feel let down by the lack of support from my sales manager
- I am not fearless and often get scared of prospecting
- I sometimes get depressed when things are not going well for me. This makes me hesitate to get on with the things I know I should be doing

Now, based on your analysis of your strong and weak points, you need to formulate an affirmation that will override your non-positive attributes in your subconscious mind.

This is the statement we arrived at from the example given above:

I (your name) am always positive, fearless and self motivated. I am proud of what I do and confident that I always achieve whatever I set out to do. I am brilliant at prospecting for new business and always make it a priority.

Notice that there are no non-positive words in that statement. Weak attributes have been turned into strong ones and linked directly to the original strong points in order to establish a close association between them.

Now take some time to write your own affirmation. Take as long as you need and rewrite it as many times as you have to until it sounds good and feels good. When you have this complete, learn it off by heart and use this in place of the affirmation you have been using for the previous six weeks.

When you carry out your visualisation exercises, see, hear and feel yourself in a situation where you are acting precisely as described in your affirmation. Within no time at all you will be that person you are seeing, hearing and feeling. Then you can start to use PDP to change any other aspects of your life. Here is another example of just how effective this can be, even in a very short period of time. It is my daughter Natasha's story.

NATASHA'S STORY

From the age of sixteen, Natasha had a dream. She wanted to get a place to study Spatial Design at Central St Martins College in London, probably one of the world's most prestigious and respected design colleges. At the appropriate time, she submitted an application along with references from her current art tutors for one of the forty places that were available. Over two thousand people applied for one of these places.

She was selected for an interview and, on the appointed day, she took her portfolio of work along to the college. The process was that her portfolio of work was to be left in a presentation room along with the other candidates' work. The selection panel would then view the candidates work in private, after which they would interview them.

Natasha's interview lasted less than five minutes. She was told that her work was simply not up to the required standard, that she had shown little or no progress over the two years that her work represented and that she would definitely not be offered a place. She left feeling totally devastated and cried uncontrollably for two days. When she had finally calmed down sufficiently for me to speak with her, I suggested she applied to the one other college in the UK that offered a spatial design course. However, she was concerned that she should have applied for a place months earlier and felt it was possibly too late. I suggested that she applied anyway and, as she had been taught to do on several occasions in the past, create an affirmation confirming her being offered a place at this college, attending and getting her degree there. She agreed to do this.

One week later, a letter arrived from Central St Martins College. It was a circular sent to everyone who had attended the interview saying that somebody had lost their portfolio of work and would they look to see if they had taken it by mistake. Natasha looked in her portfolio for the first time since that day she had been rejected and found the missing work mixed up with her own. She telephoned the college, told them she had the missing work and asked if there was any possibility that her work had been judged on the standard of this other person's work. They told her that was not possible, that was the end of the matter and would she please post the missing work back to them. Simultaneously, and unbeknownst to her, one of her current tutors had also written to Central St Martins expressing his surprise that she had been rejected for a place.

Two weeks later, she received two letters in the post. The first she opened was from the college she had applied to for an interview, offering her a date to attend. "You see", I said proudly, "affirmations always work". She smiled sweetly and said "Dad, I have to be honest. I wasn't affirming for an interview at that college. I was still affirming and visualising getting a place at Central St Martins." Then she opened the second envelope. It was a letter from Central St Martins saying that they believed they may have judged her application based on someone else's work and would she please telephone for another interview. That took place a week later and they were so impressed with her work that she was offered an unconditional place. Three years later she obtained her degree.

Two years on from then, and after working as a intern in several magazines, she applied for a position as a stylist for Living Etc., the UK's best selling interior design magazine. Eight hundred other people also applied for that position, many of them far more qualified and experienced than Natasha, but she got the job—probably because she was the only one who affirmed and visualised getting it.

Whatever else it is you want to attain, create an affirmation that describes the situation as if you have already achieved it. Repeat that, as you have been with your previous affirmations, and experience miracles in your life too.

Summary

The Secrets To Success

"You are today where your thoughts have brought you; you will be tomorrow where your thoughts take you"
James Allen — Author of As a Man Thinketh

Do you recognize the following person from this brief biography?

- He lost his business at age 31.
- He was defeated in a legislative race at 32.
- He failed again in business at age 34.
- His childhood sweetheart died when he was 35 years old.
- He had a nervous breakdown at 36 years of age.
- He lost a state election at age 38.
- He lost a congressional race at age 43, another at age 46 and yet another at age 48.
- He failed to become a state senator when he was 55.
- He failed to become elected vice-president at aged 56.
- He lost another senatorial race at age 58.
- He was elected President of the United States of America at age 60.

His name was Abraham Lincoln.

Abraham Lincoln had the three attributes that every great achiever has to have in order to be successful. Those attributes are COMMITMENT, DETERMINATION AND PERSISTENCE.

The following is a story about someone you will definitely not have heard of. He is a salesperson called Albert Weinstock. I was first introduced to Albert when I was asked to coach twenty-five of the

169

top salespeople working with a large financial services organisation. This was the top twenty-five of three thousand financial salespeople, so you can imagine they were very successful people already. Albert, however, stood out like a sore thumb. Whilst the other twenty-four salespeople were extremely well dressed, looked very fit and were very articulate, the politest thing I can say about Albert was that he was the complete opposite of that. Nevertheless, based on his sales production, Albert had certainly earned his place in the top twenty-five.

When I asked the twenty-four how they would explain in fifteen seconds what they did for their clients, they had some very interesting and sophisticated ways of describing themselves. One example was: "I help people minimise the effects of taxation during their lifetimes and ensure that as much of their estate as possible is passed on to their families on their death rather than into the government coffers." Another was "I help people to plan their financial affairs so that they are able to retire ten years earlier than they would otherwise be able to do so." Albert's was "I sell life insurance, pensions and savings plans".

I was fascinated by Albert and in one of the coffee breaks I sat down with Albert to find out more about him. It transpired that he had worked in the postal services for many years until his mother became widowed and quite ill and he was unable to care for her properly on his postman's salary. He had applied for several other jobs without success when he heard that very good incomes could be made in financial services, and as it was commission only based, they were not too fussy who they took on. He told me that after the interview when he was offered a position and found out what he could earn if he was successful, he became absolutely committed and determined to succeed in his new career. He sold his car and everything else he thought he could do without and raised enough money to be able to keep himself and his mother for three months whilst he was learning his new trade.

Albert tried many of the sophisticated approaches used by the top sellers in his company but was not comfortable with them, and he failed dismally. Then he decided to try a totally different approach, one that he himself invented. This approach quickly earned him the nickname 'Tower Block Albert'. This is what he did.

Albert took a bus or train to the nearest tower block of apartments. He would take the lift to the top floor and then walk down and ring the bell on every front door. If it was answered he would say "Good afternoon Sir (or Madam). My name is Albert Weinstock, representing the (XYZ) Company. I sell life insurance, pensions and investment plans. I am here today introducing myself and making appointments for next Wednesday with people who would like to buy one or other of those. Would you like to make an appointment with me too?"

I have to say that I cringed at this approach, but the fact is that by the time Albert had reached the ground floor he had always made at least four appointments, and when he went back, he sold to every single one of them. That was Albert's sole method of prospecting for new customers. He never even asked for referrals and Albert had been doing that for seven years. I consider that one of the most extraordinary examples of commitment, determination and persistence, and a lesson for us all.

Think back to any time in your life when you were absolutely, totally committed to achieve something. I know you achieved it because absolute commitment is incompatible with failure.

Think back to any time in your life when you were absolutely determined to achieve something. I know you achieved it because absolute determination is incompatible with failure.

Think back to any time in your life when you persistently worked towards achieving something. I know you achieved it because persistence is absolutely incompatible with failure.

If you follow everything I have shown you in this book and are committed, determined and persistent in applying these techniques, then it is not possible that you will not double your sales.

I will leave you with one final thought:

The greatest amongst us are no different to the rest. They simply take a few steps each day and march towards their goals. And the days go by and the weeks go by and the months go by, and one day they wake up and find themselves in a place called Extraordinary!

I look forward to seeing you there.

SIGN UP FOR BRUCE KING'S

FREE NEWSLETTER AND SALES TIPS AT

WWW.BRUCEKING.CO.UK

Printed in the United States
128461LV00002B/15/P